# SEAN P. THE READER

## A Collection of Thoughts

© Kofi Piesie Research Team Same Tree Different Branch

Kofi Piesie/Mossi Warrior Clan

Copyright 2024 by Same Tree Different Branch Publishing

All rights reserved. No Part of this book may be reproduced or transmitted in any form or by any means, electronic or mechanical, including photocopying, recordings, or by any information storage and retrieval systems without the written permission of the publisher.

Printed in the United States of America

**ISBN** 979-8-9896372-5-6

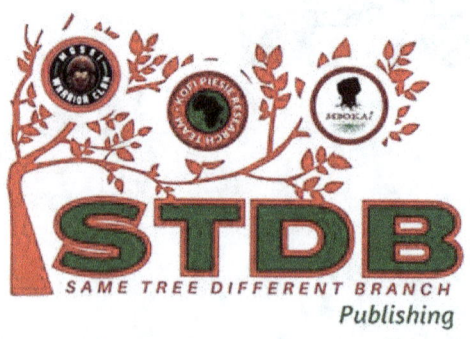

# The Anatomy of a Book

By: Seanathan Polidore, M.S.P.

# Table of Content

New Foreword: Kofi Piesie……………..6

OG Foreword: Keith Nickerson………....12

Prologue: Carlos Garcia………………15

Introduction: Dr. Ashley Wade…………..22

Chapter 1: Reading Is Fun for The Mental (Fundamental)……………………….27

Chapter 2: Mind Travel (Outta This World)……………………………….33

Chapter 3: Increase Your Vocabulary (Got Bars?) ……………………………….37

Chapter 4: Improve School Performance (Keep Ya A Game)………………….43

Chapter 5: Learn More about Your Rich History………………………………51

Chapter 6: About the Author……………..59

Chapter 7: Table of Contents……………..63

Chapter 8: Acknowledgements…………...67

Chapter 9: Foreword……………………70

Chapter 10: Introduction……………….74

Chapter 11: Afterword........................78

OG Afterword: Versana Polidore (AKA Mama Vee) ....................................81

Afterword Remix: Reggie Bailey (AKA Reggie Reads) ...................................84

An Ode to Reading: Tamekia Rasheed...........................................90

Points to Consider............................ 93

Reading Tip: Check the Footage............96

# NEW FOREWORD

## New Foreword: Kofi Piesie

I have been tasked to write the foreword for this book. So, I want to thoroughly break down what makes up a book's body. I always like starting any topic with a working definition, so let's define the word anatomy.

According to Britannica, anatomy is a field in the biological sciences concerned with the identification and description of the body structures of living things. Gross anatomy involves the study of major body structures by dissection and observation and, in its narrowest sense, is concerned only with the human body.

https://www.britannica.com/science/anatomy

With all that said, it simply means anatomy is the description of living things. It is a branch of biology and medicine. People who study anatomy study the body, how it is made up, and how it works.

 Many parts make up the body of a book, concerning the identification and description of the body structure that makes it a living thing that comes to life through its layout, format, and pages. Understanding the anatomy of a book is not just for bibliophiles or those in the publishing industry; it's a fascinating glimpse into a world where form and function harmoniously intersect.

The Author, Seanathan Polidore, covers the anatomy of a book very well in this book, but let's look at the biological makeup of a Book.

The Book consists of the Book Cover, Spine, Endpaper, Title Page, Copyright Page, Dedication, Foreword, Introduction, Table of Contents, Chapters, Footnotes and Endnotes, Appendices, Glossary, Bibliography, and Index.

I want to compare each part of a book to show how each section operates just like each human part that makes up a living thing,


- **Book Cover** ↔ Skin: The book cover, like skin, is the first line of defense and presentation. It protects the contents within and gives the first impression.

- **Spine** ↔ Human Spine: The book's spine keeps the structure intact, just as the human

spine supports the body and enables it to maintain its posture.
- **Endpapers** ↔ Ears: Endpapers are not immediately noticeable but contribute to the book's overall aesthetic, similar to ears, which play a subtle yet essential role in perception.

- **Title Page** ↔ Face: The title page, displaying the book's title and author, represents the book's identity, akin to a human face.

- **Copyright Page** ↔ DNA/Genetic Code: This section contains unique publication and legal details, much like DNA, which carries the unique genetic information of an individual.

- **Dedication** ↔ Heart: The dedication is often a personal and heartfelt message from the author, reflecting the emotional and central role of the heart.

- **Foreword** ↔ Forebrain: The forward, often providing insight or context, can be likened to the forebrain, responsible for complex cognitive processes.

- **Introduction** ↔ Mouth: Serving as the entry point to the book's content, the introduction is like the mouth, which is the entryway for nutrition and speech.

- **Table of Contents** ↔ Brain: This section organizes the book's structure, like the brain, which organizes and coordinates bodily functions.

- **Chapters, Headings, and Subheadings** ↔ Bones and Muscles: They provide the book's framework and organization, just like bones and muscles structure and move the body.

- **Footnotes and Endnotes** ↔ Peripheral Nervous System: These notes give supplementary information, akin to the peripheral nervous system conveying additional sensory and motor information.

- **Appendices** ↔ Appendix: The appendices offer additional, often non-essential material, paralleling the appendix in the human body, which has a supplementary role.

- **Glossary** ↔ Memory: A glossary helps in understanding specific terms, like how memory aids in recalling and understanding information.

- **Bibliography/References** ↔ Digestive System: Like the digestive system, which extracts nutrients from food, a bibliography extracts and lists sources of information.

- **Index** ↔ Nervous System: The index helps in quickly locating information, analogous to the nervous system, which transmits signals rapidly throughout the body.
In this comparison, each book section and human body part are vital to their respective whole, working together to create something functional and meaningful. Each section in creating a book from the womb of your mind is important in bringing the book to life.

# FOREWORD

Foreword: Keith Nickerson

It is a tall task, a momentous undertaking, instructing how to READ a BOOK properly. To advise, one has to put in work and hours of study to achieve mastery. Many begin the mission, find it impossible, and self-destruct in five seconds before finishing the FOREWORD. The seed fell on a well-trodden path and was eaten by birds.

PERCEPTION is essential, and the end may seem nearer than actuality. The adventure begins with enthusiasm. A few White Whales, Ravens, and Pearls were captured or discovered, precious items only for a moment. Zest fades, as does zeal. The seed fell on rocky ground, never taking root.

Verification is involved when instructing before following them off a bridge. The rope you're thrown may slip and wind up around your neck. The seed fell amongst weeds and thorns; the crop grew, but dense weeds choked with curiosity. Reading became unessential.

Qualifications aren't honorary; they demand person-hours, possibly 10,000. Nose to the grind, sponging information, memorizing, retaining, filing, and LEARNING, he constantly hones his God-given gift. This seed fell on good soil, and the harvest:

SEANATHAN QUINN POLIDORE

DESIRE can be CERTIFIED, and it's WITNESSED.

PASSION can't be injected; either you got it, or you don't!

LOVE does not DOMINATE; reading assists to CULTIVATE.

FRIENDSHIP is fleeting; my life changed forever in the summer of 2017.

I was taught that it's as essential to READ as WRITE!

The author of this project is more than qualified; references need not be verified, and as a literary griot, he is industry-wide certified. Open your mind and allow a different slant to alter the ERUDITUION process. Completing this project will enable readers to expand their comprehension and tap into untapped mental strengths.

ENJOY!

# PROLOGUE

## Prologue: Carlos Garcia

"I owe everything I am and everything I will ever be to books" - Gary Paulsen.

Who knows why some start the habit of reading books and some don't?

For me, the love of reading started when I was very young. I remember being transported to these different worlds when reading "The Adventures of Huckleberry Finn" by Mark Twain and "Goosebumps" books by R.L Stine. I still remember being scared to ask my mother for $2 a month so that she could buy me the latest "Goosebumps" book. Her saying yes to me is still one of my favorite memories. These books fueled my passion for reading, and that passion still burns brighter than ever. Here are some reasons why I continue to read books to this day.

### Books as mentors

"The reading of all good books is like a conversation with the finest minds of the past centuries" - Rene Descartes.

I was raised by a single mother who worked tirelessly to put food on the table for six kids, myself being the oldest. I feel like I did not have many mentors growing up. No accurate role models for teaching me the ways of the world. This is where books saved me. Books written by men and women I have never met became my mentors. In his book "Do You," Russell Simmons taught me not to follow trends and to wear clothing that never goes out of style. He also recommended the book "The Power of Now" by Ekhart Tolle. Ekhart taught me to let go of the past, not fear the future, and focus on the moment. Chris Widener, who wrote "The Slight Edge," taught me to read ten pages daily to develop the habit of reading. The list goes on. I have been fortunate enough to learn from people much smarter than me. All I had to do was pick up their book, read what they had to teach, and apply it to my life. You may feel like you don't have any mentors in your life. Maybe you are too fearful to ask someone to mentor you formally. Remember, a mentor is waiting for you to pick up their book so they can impress upon you what they have learned during their journey called life.

Your next aha moment

"The book you don't read won't help" - Jim Rohn.

Reading books is great because you never know when you will come across a passage that will give you an Aha moment. This moment of insight has the power to revolutionize your entire life. After reading "The Power of Now, " I decided to move from Massachusetts to San Diego, and it helped me build the courage to leave the safe place I called home and take a giant leap of faith across the country. After reading "Rich Dad Poor Dad," I decided to buy a condo during one of the worst recessions in my lifetime. When I read the phrase "You get what you tolerate," it completely changed the way I looked at the world, and I started reassessing what I would and would not tolerate. Many great ideas and insights are waiting for you to read them. The next aha moment with the power to change your life could be just one book away.

Books help build relationships.

"You're the average of the five people you spend the most time with" - Jim Rohn.

Reading books is a great way to make friends and build relationships. It is a great way to meet like-minded people and get different perspectives on a book you both might be reading. I became friends with Seanathan because of a book. One of my coworkers noticed I was reading a book called "Brainwashed" by Tom Burrell. She sent Seanathan a picture of the cover to see if he had read it, and it turns out he had. From there, we started group texting and discussing the books we were reading.

Six years later, we still communicate often, and I consider him a very close friend. What is crazier is that we still have not met in person. Such is the power of books. I recommend joining a book club near you or starting a book club. It is a great way to meet like-minded people. Here is a tip for those in the workforce. Find out what the managers and leaders of your organization are reading and make it a point to read that book. Now, you have something in common that you can discuss, and they will kindly share the insights they gained from the book. This is a great way to build rapport and relationships with upper management. You never know what relationships will grow from the mutual connection of reading a book. Who knows, you might even have the opportunity to write the prologue of your friend's book.

The application of knowledge is power.

"The great aim of education is not knowledge but action." — Herbert Spencer.

You have probably heard the phrase "Knowledge is Power." I will take that a step further and state that the *application* of knowledge is power. You could read all the books in the world, and if you do not apply the knowledge you have gained, what use is it? For example, I'm currently reading a book on negotiation called "Never Split The Difference" by Chris Voss. If I do not practice and apply the tips and techniques taught, I've only gained a better understanding of how negotiations work. I will not become a better negotiator because I understand how negotiations work better. It is not until I apply and practice the techniques, I have learned from the book that knowledge becomes power. The real power is using what you have learned to grow and improve at whatever you try to achieve. That is why this book is so important. It teaches techniques that help turn the knowledge you gain from books into power you can apply in your everyday life.

Books are the great equalizer in life. It does not matter where you grew up or what race you are. If you know how to read, you can take advantage of all the benefits of books.

Books can provide you with a mentor, help build relationships, and provide life-changing insights for years to come. It is up to you to decide whether you are going to develop the habit of reading or not, and I hope you pick the former.

# INTRODUCTION REMIX

Introduction Remix: Dr. Ashley Wade

Good People,
I am so excited for you! The information and guides written in this book are like a cheat code to a complex video game. It's similar to learning how to look at a landscape and admire the parts and the whole of the experience. Sean is an excellent teacher, and it shows how he presents The Anatomy of a Book. First of all, who thinks to actually introduce this skill to readers? This is a necessary skill for all that they don't teach you in English class. The ability to read and, more importantly, study is a virtue that not many people actually experience, and the reason may be that most people read for leisure. Although there is nothing wrong with reading for leisure, you can elevate personally and professionally if you can learn how to study. But foundationally, you have to learn how and why books are put together the way they are. Consider the author's perspective and intentions. What do they want me to know when I open this book? What information, feelings, and expressions do they want me to walk away with? And the ultimate question is, how does

all that benefit me? Will I develop psychologically? Will I experience relief or personal freedom? Will I learn character-building skills? Will this book add cultural context to my understanding of the world, myself, and my place in it? Authors consider so much as they build and create books for readers. I appreciate that because there is no way the author can predict who will be inspired to pick up their book and read it. So, if you do pick up a book, be open to whatever messages, stories, and guidelines are presented in the way they are presented. Receive the intention, process it through your psyche, and decide what makes sense and resonates with YOU. Also, keep in mind that you get the maximum benefit(s) of reading by understanding the parts and purpose(s) of each part of a book. Sometimes, we miss out on the best gems by skipping certain sections because we have not been taught about the importance of each part. At the end of the day, it's all about Knowledge Acquisition and Education. As you read this book, I want you to know in advance that by completing this book, you are securing a lifelong analytical skill in your toolbox of life resources.

Welcome to your next level of elevation; I introduce you to "The Anatomy of a Book," written and curated by the Great Sean P. Peace and Blessings.

Continue to Seek and: Be Light, So You Can Be You and Max That Shit Out!

Dr. Ashley Wade
 Pharmacist, Author, Griotte.

**Part One: The Benefits of Reading**

In this book segment, I will share some of the beautiful benefits of reading. Once again, all of the novella books I have been releasing lately come from a compilation of speeches and notes I have presented over my twelve-year public speaking career. For this book, I was allowed to speak to a group of teens about the importance of reading for the S.M.I.L.E. summer program in Lafayette, La, in 2017. I have done countless social media videos, and PowerPoint presentations about why I choose to read so much and what I feel has been a payoff to that diligent practice. In the first chapters of this book, I will share with you just a few things that have kept me turning the pages night and day for the past twenty years of my life.

# CHAPTER 1

Reading Is Fun for The Mental
(Fundamental)

## Chapter 1: Reading Is Fun for The Mental (Fundamental)

"Education is not the filling of a pail, but the lighting of a fire."

As a kid of the 80s, a powerful slogan displayed on T.V. to encourage us to read more was, Reading is Fundamental. It was a great marketing strategy; to some, it hit home but missed the target for many of us. We all knew that the ability to read was important without question, but for some of us, it was flat-out boring, so we did not want to do it. Some of you reading this book feel the same feeling right now. Well, let me tell you that thinking back on that slogan, I think they would have reached a wider audience if they could have made us realize that reading could be F.U.N. for the Mental. What do you mean by that, Sean? You see, people have the perception that reading is a passive activity. Like plainly sit in one spot and let the words casually come to you off the page. That may be true for a particular segment of people, which is fine, but when discussing reading, I talk about a very aggressive hands-on activity. First, I would encourage you to read books the way you watch T.V. Most people do not watch the same shows on the same channel night and day. We naturally change the channel and performance based on our mood. You may watch the football game for one minute and then go to your favorite YouTube channel next. You follow that with the Discovery channel if you love science like me, followed by some scary movies! I try to read my books in the same fashion. Now, this may be more of an advanced suggestion to some, but if you can follow along with more than one book at a time, I suggest you give it a shot. For countless years I have been reading about three to four books at once, and I change them up at a moment's notice depending on my mood. With this technique, you will be more involved and engaged in the content because you are reading something you WANT to read instead of reading something you are being made to read. This can be an exhilarating adventure if you allow yourself to open up to it. Not to mention, when you start to read multiple books that are vastly different, your brain begins to make connections in the stories that not many people around you have picked up on. I will explore how this improves your academic performance later in the publication. So, the next time you feel yourself drifting off reading or you find yourself reading the same lines repeatedly because you are losing focus, try changing the channel (mentally.)

Engage the Content

Another way that reading can be Fun for the mentally is by engaging the content. Now, Sean, what do you mean by that? I am talking about the art of attacking the pages in the book with pens, highlighters, markers, sticky notes, colorful tabs, etc. This is one of the most exciting parts of reading for me. Nothing feels better than giving a new book a ton of tattoos! Small disclaimer. I am speaking directly about the books YOU OWN for this book section! NOT LIBRARY BOOKS! If you are a youth reading this, ask your parents to take you to the stationary section of your local Office Depot, Office Max, Walmart, etc.

Try to find stickers and colors that speak to you. Find the perfect pen you would love to write with. Hunt down the type of highlighter color that will make the essential words stick to your memory. This could be an adventure all within itself, let alone what you will do WITH these materials. Now, for the moment, we have all been waiting for it. Get your favorite book of the moment, and when anything you read is a mind-blowing idea for you, I want you to take those highlighters and highlight the exact line that grabs your attention. Now, as you are reading, if you can, I want you to try to use a different color per paragraph so that it can jump out to your mind off the page. Next, as you are reading, please take your sticky notes and write down people, places, or dates that stand out in your mind. Also, do not be afraid to write in the book's margins over, under, and on the side of the text. I try my best to use every bit of the page available if what I am reading is that powerful to me and makes my mind draw connections to other things. As you read, imagine having a back-and-forth conversation with the author. This is not meant to be a one-way monologue. On some of your sticky notes, jot down questions that you are thinking about what you are reading. Make your questions as if you were in an interview with the writer. Also, try to guess what will happen next. What will the characters do? Who will be victorious? Will someone die? Will there be another book written to follow it up?

All these activities and many more like it keep reading fresh and fun to participate in. You will also increase your comprehension of what you are reading and fully grasp the content. When you finish the chapter, sit back and look at the wide range of colors you used to highlight, and the various color stick notes scattered over the pages. Now, this is a work of art that jumps out and grabs you. This is NOT a passive activity. This is a sword fight!

"When trouble strikes, head to the library. You will either be able to solve the problem or simply have something to read as the world crashes down on you."

# CHAPTER 2

Mind Travel (Outta This World)

## Chapter 2: Mind Travel (Outta This World)

If you have read some of my other works, you will realize that besides the topic of mentorship, one of my favorite subjects to speak about is the importance of travel to transform your mind. There is no more incredible feeling for me than waking up in a new place and inhaling fresh air that feels new to my lungs. Regarding reading, if you cannot afford to get in a car or plane and take a trip abroad, know that you can go anywhere you WANT IN YOUR MIND! My favorite rapper of all time is Jay Z (that's right, debate me on it), and my favorite line from him of all time comes from his first album, Reasonable Doubt. On his track, Dead Presidents, he has a bar where he says, "Lock My body/ Can't trap my mind." I love this line so much, and it sticks with me so profoundly because he expressed in his literary genius that you could try to do whatever you please to his physical body. However, he could do whatever and go wherever he wanted mentally. I have had tough jobs in an unforgiving environment, and I would say that the only way I could endure such conditions was due to my ability to escape mentally while I worked my hands to the bone. How does this apply to reading Sean? For some people, you may not be crazy about the city where you currently live, or maybe your family is not in a position to take you on trips all over the world. If you start to read books, articles, and journals about foreign places, you can gain the knowledge of a well-traveled person. Of course, nothing replaces real experiences, but in the meantime, this will give you a big leg up on your peers who do not tackle this type of reading and investigation. A better understanding of how the world works outside the city you are in every day will help you make better life choices and increase your sense of the possibilities beyond your city lights.

I speak more on the importance of travel in my book Expanding Your Vision, and a large part of expanding your vision of yourself comes from going to places outside of what has been comfortable to you. One of the advantages of reading that you have over physical travel is, once again, that you can go anywhere in your mind. No…Really. Anywhere! You can travel overseas; you can travel to different planets. You can even leave this Galaxy if you want by way of books! No travel agent in the world can offer you that.

The tip of this chapter will be to sit down and think of a place you have always wanted to visit. Think of something you may have heard about in a song, seen in a video, or observed in a movie. Do not forget that this place must not be restricted to Earth. Next, please go to your local library, school library, or bookstore and try to find as many books as you can in that location. You want something with as many pictures and descriptions as possible on this subject. Take note of the significant landmarks and historical points in the publication. Imagine being in these places. What would you want to do in this place? How would you spend your time?

"Travel is fatal to narrow-mindedness." – Keith Nickerson

# CHAPTER 3

Increase Your Vocabulary (Got Bars?)

Chapter 3: Increase Your Vocabulary (Got Bars?)

Now, one of my favorite reading aspects is increased vocabulary. When you read books that challenge you, and not just the books that barely have words on the page and are full of pictures, your mind starts to take in and recall these words subconsciously. That means whether you want to or not, the more broadly you read, the more your mind picks up words and adds them to your vocabulary toolbox. Yes, I said it, vocabulary toolbox. What is that, you may ask? Let us look at this example I use with young guys all the time. As I mentioned in chapter two, I love hip-hop. I always have and always will. When I meet young guys who want to be rappers, I always make it a point to ask them if they have a dictionary or thesaurus app on their smartphone. %100 of the time, they say no, unfortunately. The example I always use with them is to imagine words like tools in a box. If we were to both try to make as many different albums as possible without using the same themes, phrases, and words. If he has 550 words in his toolbox and I have 2,500 words in my toolbox, who could make the most albums without sounding the same over and over again? The answer would be me. The more you read, the more words you add to your mental toolbox to give you the ability to create and build more things and have options. If you are rapping, singing, or writing, you do not want to describe a car as just a red car. You want to tell the car so vividly that the listener can see the exact make, model, type of red, what type of gloss is on the paint job, and how the car feels and smells. As another one of my favorite rappers, 50 Cent, said, you want to use words to paint pictures. Think of some of the rappers with the longest and most successful careers, and most of those names are people who have a good grasp of the English language, whether they graduated from school or not.

You see, learning goes way beyond the walls of the classroom. Most of these guys were very well-read and well-traveled, so when it came time for them to put words together in the booth, they had very large toolboxes to construct. Think of Kendrick, Tupac, Nas, Jay Z, Biggie, Loaded Lux, Locksmith, Tech Nine, Talib, Mos Def, Common, T.I., Jill Scott, Badu, Indie Aire, I could go on (readers tip: Search some of the names listed that you DON'T know). If you YouTube some of their lyrics or study them in interviews, it becomes apparent that they read... A LOT. Artists such as Nas, Tupac, Jay Z, and Gza from the Wu-Tang clan have used their lyrics in college classrooms to be broken down in writing and English class for their poetical wizardry with words.

Most of the books I write are written with youth in mind or adults who are not big on reading, and I am trying to encourage them to read, so I purposely try not to use powerful words that would push some away. Now, the books I read in my free time are primarily scholarly works by doctors. These books can be extensive, and their use of long and unheard-of words to describe things can be displayed throughout their publications. One book comes to my mind as I write, and that is Medical Apartheid. The author of this book has an extensive vocabulary, and I had to keep a dictionary close by while reading her work.

My tip for this chapter goes back to the highlighters and markers you purchased in chapter one. I want you to pick up your favorite book, and as you read it, I want you to highlight or underline any word you come across that you do not know. After you highlight it, I want you to get a dictionary or use your handy dandy smartphone and google the word. Define it and try to make a note on one of your sticky pads or jot it down in the margin of the book itself (MAKE SURE IT IS NOT A LIBRARY BOOK!) The more you do this practice, the more it will become second nature to you. Once again, we are doing the active reading and attacking the page. This activity is yet another way to make the information stick to your mind. I cannot explain it scientifically, and even if I could, I probably would not do it for the sake of this book, but when you highlight things and note them, your mind recalls them faster and easier. Before you know it, as time passes, you will have notebooks full of words to look back over and even practice using in a sentence with friends. One of my favorite things is learning a new comment and trying to use it in everyday conversation with family and friends as effortlessly as saying Hot and Spicy.

You will be surprised at the looks and reactions you get from people. If you have an eBook form of a book, you can hold your finger on the words you want to look up, and the definition will pop up on your screen. I would still advise you to get a small notepad and write the words down to glance over from time to time. It helps you to recall the words better in the future if you handwrite them. Increasing your vocabulary allows you to express your exact thoughts and feelings to the world better. Invest in your toolbox.

"You don't see with your eyes; you see with your brain. The more words your brain has, the more things you can see."

– KRS-One, one of the Godfathers of Rap

# CHAPTER 4

Improve School Performance (Keep Ya A Game)

## Chapter 4: Improve School Performance (Keep Ya A Game)

The most important thing to understand about reading more is improving school performance. Your performance in school may be one of the most life-shaping things that will happen in your life and can set the tone for how you will experience your adult life. So, making excellent grades in school early on is something that you want to get a handle on with a sense of urgency. Several studies have shown that students who consistently read outside their school curriculum scored higher in ALL subjects on their achievement tests. When you think about the most standardized tests, they usually involve what element? That's right, much reading! Even if it is the math portion of the trial, if you cannot read word problems correctly and understand what operations are being asked of you, it can significantly impact your chances of scoring high in that arena. The reading comprehension portion is straightforward here. What do they want students to display? The ability to read a passage, recall significant characters and events, and show understanding of what they just read. The more a student uses some of the tools I laid out earlier in the book, the more practice they get at doing just that. Students who love to read have more engagement with the lessons and the teacher, making them pay much more attention to what is being disseminated. Being more active and interested in the subjects will give you a higher percentage of success than your classmates, who are daydreaming with their head on the desk.

I can personally attest to the power of reading in improving my academic ability. As a child, I hate to admit it, but I was a very mediocre student at best. Not because something was mentally wrong but because I had a substantial lack of interest in school, and to top it all off, I was not crazy about reading outside of my assigned schoolwork. As a young man of my generation, I could think of nothing better to do with my downtime than a chance to play ball anywhere one was bouncing. The last thing on my mind would be to sit still and read a book. It is no wonder that as I got older and my love for reading grew my grades in college began to take flight. I felt like I had a cheat code versus my classmates, and you would think I knew things they did not. Many times, I did. The amount of outside reading I had done before entering school and the wide range of topics I had partaken in made me more well-rounded about a more significant number of issues than most students in my classes. I owe ALL my academic success to the skill of reading. I owe the honor of being an author and all of the spoils that have come to that world. I owe my public speaking career directly to literacy because to go on that mic and have something to give means you have to have something inside of your mind worth giving. I got all of those gems during my reading. You could consider this book an ode to reading.

Increased Concentration

Students who read in their free time experienced increased focus and concentration compared to their peers who did not. We live in a day and time where attention is far between in a world filled with distractions at every glance. From the moment we open our eyes, we are bombarded with social media, T.V., video games, etc. To have the ability to sit still and focus on reading for extended periods uninterrupted is a supreme skill to possess and will serve you greatly in various aspects of your life. Over the years, people have had the misconception that "multitasking" will help them to be more effective in their endeavors, but they could not be further from the truth. Concentrating and zeroing in on one task enables you to execute at a higher level than trying to split your focus. What is an excellent way to practice this skill? You guessed it. Reading!

Usage tip: Master the Clock

I want you to go on Amazon and order a 5-minute hourglass. They were very cheap. When reading, I want you to put away your phone and other distracting devices. Flip the hourglass and begin reading. As the moments go by and your mind may start to drift, look up at the sand escaping. Focus back down on the content. Before you know it, five minutes will come and go. Then you will feel like I could have read more than that in five minutes, and you flip the hourglass over again. I have used this method to start many nights of studying, and an hour of reading time has gone by in a flash. One five-minute flip at a time.

Focusing on the book and the sand will help you sharpen your concentration on the material vs. playing with your phone or watching T.V. as you read. This tip may seem incredibly simple, and it is, but it is also highly effective at helping you to increase your concentration and get more reading done in an allotted time. I started using my timer for tasks beyond reading around my house because I realized how much timelier I was than before. All of this technology we have now to improve our lives can sometimes be a hindrance. You have to go back to some of the oldest tools to make gains at this time.

Enhanced Analytical Thinking

The students who engaged in reading in their downtime increased their ability to analyze information, visualize what they read, conceptualize, and solve simple to complex problems using their given information. With most people making a large percentage of their life choices based on social media posts, having the ability to read something and decipher fact from fiction could mean life and death. Daily, we see adults quickly glance at a title on a post and rush to share it before reading the post or article, or they comment on something they have no idea about. This can make a person look very foolish and cause unnecessary conflict that could have been avoided if they had the skills to analyze and properly judge what they THOUGHT they saw. Critical thinking and analytical skills will separate you from most of your peers by a long shot.

Increased Memory

Clinical studies have shown that brain-stimulating activity from reading helps to decrease cognitive decline in older people versus other activities in their lifetime. Reading into older age has led to protecting a person up to %30 compared to nonreaders in their peer group. Reading also helped to decrease dementia risk significantly by engaging in intellectual activities daily, such as reading newspapers, magazines, journals, books, etc. According to Hong Kong, even if you pick up the habit of reading later on in life, it can still have a significant impact on preserving your brain function and memory.

I mentioned active reading in chapter one, which goes hand in hand with increasing your memory. Highlighting, underlining, making small notes on the subject, and doing further research helps embed it deeply into your memory. You also help your mind to form connections to other things and bring associations to topics that may seem unrelated on the surface, but they spark your memory once mentioned.

Usage tips for this chapter are color-coded highlighting. Use yellow boxes to symbolize the word choice or vocabulary used by the author that you find fascinating. Circle in pink to mark the story's important events, plot development, or progressions. Use the color blue and mark questions that you may have in group or class discussions. Use the color orange to mark characters and text connections you make as you are going along with the story. Use green to underline moments in the book that you may have loved or hated. Use red exclamation points to mark conflicts between characters or conflicts that you find in writing. Lastly, double underline in purple to keep literary elements or devices. Using these types of annotation skills, you will develop strong critical reading skills and the ability to comprehend what it is that you chose to read highly.

# CHAPTER 5

Learning Your Rich History (His Story)

## Chapter 5: Learning Your Rich History (His Story)

"Self-knowledge will lead to Self-Mastery."

One of the fascinating benefits of reading is learning more about my culture and myself through the books I digest. Yes, I try my best to write my books in a fashion where people from all backgrounds can relate to the lessons, but I am a black man through and through. As a black man, it is sad to say, but the reality is that you will often not learn your true history through traditional schools, churches, organizations, and other institutions. This is where your self-study skills will be of the utmost importance. From preschool through my master's degree, I can confidently say that I received very minimal Black history in school besides the old, recycled figures they give us year in and year out. It wasn't until my mid-twenties that I began to dig into books with people who looked like myself on the cover that I started to get this deep yearning in my chest to learn more and more history of Black people.

The specific book that I started with was the biography of Huey P. Newton, the leader of the Black Panther Party for Defense. I later would go on to read Assata Shakur, Geronimo Pratt, and countless other figures I had never heard of before. Their incredible stories motivated and empowered me in my day-to-day life. When I decided to read the autobiography of Malcolm X, my life would be changed forever. In this book, my mentor began to personally guide me and pour into me additional lessons that went beyond the pages of that text. We started to read and study black history day and night for years, picking apart stories and connecting dots to events happening in current times. I learned more in this three- to four-year period than in all of my years in formal school, in my opinion. I learned critical thinking, how to use logic, how to read between the lines, and how to fill in what was not there. I learned the art of writing and the power of words during this period. I always feel I owe my entire college journey to my self-study of African American history. After the intense years of reading and the assignments my mentor gave me, college schoolwork felt almost like a breeze in comparison.

Reading my history gave me an understanding of who the original people in the world were, where they were from, and how they lived their lives before slavery. I also learned that our culture created math, language, writing, sciences, astronomy, etc. For most of my time as a student in my childhood, I found it hard to connect myself to the content because it was painted as if everyone else in the world did important things besides people who looked like me. I guess in my subconscious, it felt like why I should even try. I always feel as if, had I known even half of the things we did as a people, I would have had more pride in my academic endeavors.

Another thing I learned from studying my history would be the downfall of some of the greatest civilizations the world has ever seen. I checked the horrible transatlantic slave trade and the ripple effect of events afterward. By studying the downfalls in our history, we get a crystal ball to help prevent some of the same future missteps if we take heed to them. Throughout biographies and journals, we find tales of boldness, intelligence, and perseverance that bend and twist our minds to conceive how our ancestors ever pulled off such feats. Reading these stories gave me pride in my race. I learned pride in my heritage and the direct bloodline I would never have known. I gained the confidence to take on any massive adventure, knowing it was in my genes to succeed and overcome all obstacles because I had a blueprint for it, and I've seen it all before.

"History is not everything, but it is a starting point. History is a clock that shows people their political and cultural time of day. It is a compass they use to find themselves on the map of human geography. It tells them where they are but, more importantly, what they must be." – Dr. John Henrik Clarke.

Usage tip for this chapter. When you start to read your culture's history, make it a point to use Google and look up the locations they mention to gain a physical idea of the places they are speaking about. I would also advise that as you read more history, ask the other members of your family or community who may have been around at that period, or maybe they even knew some family members before them who went through the particular episode in history. I have been using this method for the past couple of years with my grandfather, and the insight you gain on a topic from someone who has experienced it is amazing versus just flatly reading about it. Plus, this helps you to increase pride and respect for your family members.

My next reading tip for this section would be to find documentaries on the topics you are reading about. Sometimes, even a short video will help the light bulb go off in your mind in ways the words on the page may not have. As you engage in more scholarly work, note the books they mention, and then go about finding and reading those works. They call this going down the rabbit hole like Alice in Wonderland. You start with an initial subject or person, and then the next thing you know, you have 12 books in front of you out of nowhere! Your journey of self-discovery will be never-ending, and every road you find will lead to yet another. Please make it a point to be a student forever.

## Part Two

In this portion of the book, I will explain the different parts of a book and why I feel it is essential for readers not to skip past them in their haste to get through a manuscript. I noticed over the years that even my avid reader friends had the habit of going to the bookstore, buying a book, and turning straight to page one. Now that's cool, and you can do that. There is no in-stone way to go about reading a book, but in my opinion, if you skip paging one in most of the books I read, you have missed up to forty pages of power-packed information. So, with that being said, I want to take my time and help you understand why you should slow down and at least glance at the other parts of the books you decide to read. For my younger readers, every book that you read at this stage in your literary journey may not have some of these portions of a book within your books. However, I still find it valuable for you to be aware of what to expect as you get older and take on more challenging reading. For my adults reading this, I pray I can ask you to dig deeper into the books on your shelves or possibly take on more complicated work shortly. Once again, reading is an activity like a scavenger hunt. You want to peek into all the nooks and find some rare finds that no one else knows about in the books they may have read.

# CHAPTER 6

About the Author

## Chapter 6: About the Author

When you initially come across a book, I first want you to turn straight to the author section. This might be the most important page to read because WHO you ALLOW to speak into your life can be dangerous if it is the wrong person. In the about the author section, you get a detailed explanation of the author's background, education, and experience, making them the authority on the subject matter. Just because an author may be a doctor on a particular topic does not give them the right to speak with total confidence in another lane. For example, I have a master's degree in the field of Psychology. If I were to write a book on curing the Coronavirus and use a nice picture of myself with a great suit and tie on saying, hey, I have a master's, and this is why you should take my word on how to cure this virus, that would be very misleading because my field of study was NOT in the world of medicine or viruses specifically. Now, this may seem like an extreme example to make my point, but if you look around T.V. and social media these days, some of the faces and voices we have are trying to dictate how we should think, feel, vote, spend money, etc. Are they experts on these topics? Did other experts on the matter vet them? Are they just giving a mic and a camera because they are "famous"? This same thought process and questioning must be used in the selected books. We live in a day and time where just about ANYBODY can print books. So, we must be mindful of the people we allow to occupy our minds. I always say that people will put a lock on their phones, lock their bank cards with codes, lock their cars and homes, but ALLOW ANYTHING into their minds!

For future writers reading this, keep this in mind when you are about to write you're about the author section because I know how easy it is to mentally not take this portion as seriously as the body of the publication you are writing. Be sure to carefully and thoroughly clarify who you are, what you have done, and what makes you the authority on the matter.

One of the best examples I could give for the author section would be Pulitzer Prize winner, Isabel Wilkerson, From the book Warmth of Other Suns. She does a great job listing the awards she was blessed to receive for her writing, the prestigious universities where she has hosted writing classes, and her parent's involvement in the great migration. So, with that last layer, she establishes why she is writing this work and what gives her the authority to report on that specific topic in depth. After reading her about the author section in her books, she more than had my confidence in her ability, and I was more than glad to purchase her products.

" T'Challa shows them WHO YOU ARE" - Black Panther's mother, Ramonda, Black Panther film.

# CHAPTER 7

Table of Contents

Chapter 7: Table of Contents

The following section I will dissect is the table of contents. If I ask most people reading this book where they can locate the table of contents and define it in their own words, I am sure they could. At this point in the book, I want to highlight a speed-reading tip I gave in my previous publications. If you pick up a random book and start reading the table of contents, you get the blueprint of what the book is about. At that point alone, you can decide whether this book is worth your money and time. The most critical speed-reading tip in the world is avoiding all the books you DO NOT need to spend your precious time reading. When I define a table of contents, I find it is formal, a list of the chapters or sections given at the front of a book. When it comes to increasing your reading enjoyment, you have to have a direct purpose for picking up a book. What am I trying to learn here? What about this interests me specifically? What will be a significant takeaway I want to walk off with? The table of contents in the book shortens that process down incredibly because if the main meat I want to take from a book is only in chapters 9, 12, and 18, you can skip the rest of it and hone in directly on those portions of the book and move on to the next time instead of reading chapters of things that you don't care about, which sounds like a horrible time reading to me! DO NOT feel handcuffed to a book just because you picked it up. It is OK not to finish a book you are not into; it is ok to read parts of a book and move on to the next. I have seen people give themselves a hard time or almost push themselves away from reading because they are in the middle of a book, they do not like it but feel some sense of commitment to that particular book. Unless it is for a school assignment or something else vital, you are NOT locked into a contract with a book!

One of the main books that comes to my mind when I think about the value of a table of contents is The 48 Laws of Power by Robert Greene. I have never seen a person maximize a table of contents like Robert Greene does. He packs so much valuable information into his table of contents. You could just read his table of contents in one of his books and have a very rough handle on the subject matter—enough to hold a conversation about it. Of course, it will vary based on the genre and level of books you read. All books will not be as in-depth as a Robert Greene book by any stretch of the imagination, but my point is that you never know what you may reveal to yourself by at least giving it an honest look.

# CHAPTER 8

Acknowledgements

# Chapter 8: Acknowledgements

As an author, the acknowledgments section of my book is vital because, in this section, I am pouring out my honor and reverence to the people that I feel are instrumental in the production of that project. Formally, when you define acknowledgments, you will find an author's or publisher's statement of indebtedness to others, typically printed at the beginning of a book. Once again, as you advance and read more scholarly work and nonfiction-type things, you will see the author list the libraries or universities they used to gather their research for the publication. Some of these scholars will shout out to a specific librarian who helped them pick further research on the subject they were writing about. They will list other contributing people who assisted them in the interview process, editing, writing, picture gathering, etc. You can learn many lessons by reading these things. You may want to look up these libraries and their online archives for your reasons. You may want to investigate some of the contributing editors or writers because they may have books of their own that they wrote in the past that could spark your attention. As always, I must advise that every single book you read may not go as deep as some of the things I have listed above, but that is the point. You will never know what is in store in this book section.

My best example of an excellent acknowledgment section would be the book Fredrick Douglas: Prophet of Freedom by David Blight. In this book, Mr. Blight explains the family he stumbled upon that happened to his extensive Douglas collection they had just been sitting on for years, and it was all the ammunition he would need to write the 600-plus page monster of a publication.

"Acknowledgement and celebration are essential to fueling passion, making people feel valid and valuable, and giving the team a real sense of progress that makes it all worthwhile."

-Dwight Frindt

# CHAPTER 9
Foreword

## Chapter 9: Foreword

The foreword of a book is sometimes one of my favorite sections of the book. You never know what a fellow scholar, a famous athlete, a family member of the author, or an expert in the field may be writing. So, it feels like bonus material in the book—like the added scenes to your favorite movie. Formally, when you define the term foreword, you find prefatory comments (as for a book) primarily when written by someone other than the author. At times, you will find the author is writing every section of the book that I am detailing him or herself, which is fine, too. When I first became a serious reader, I noticed that when I read the work of my favorite scholar, one of his great buddies wrote the foreword. Then I would look up that person and find out he wrote some fantastic books, too. Then, as I read those books, I realized that someone else did the editing work in these books. So, I went on to look up that person, and he had a catalog of books as well. It was a giant rabbit hole of information. This is another example of being an active reader. You become like a private investigator digging for more and more connections to the work you are reading. Within the book's foreword, the writer gives you a snapshot of their thoughts on the subject and what they hope the reader will take away from it. This is like giving you a small trailer before you get to page one.

I have had the privilege and the honor to write a few forewords for a few buddies of mine, and I tell you, it was almost more challenging to write these forewords than to write my entire books! I only say that because when you are asked to write a piece for someone else's project, you do not want to come across as if you are trying to take over the project. So, there is a fine line you want to tiptoe. You want your words to be fire and strike the right note but fall into place with the words the author is about to lay out for the rest of the book. Usually, a foreword may be between 2 to 5 pages, give or take. In larger books, I have seen some go up to 40 pages just in FOREWORD alone!

As a side note to my future writers, writing a foreword, introduction, or afterword for another writer can be a great way to get your feet wet and experience the publishing process without carrying the total weight of writing a complete book yourself. As you noticed, in all of my books, I have tried my best to feature people who have never published a book before to give them a shot at feeling what it is like to have your name in print.

For my example of a special foreword, I turn to one of my favorite books, Michelle Alexander's New Jim. Cornel West does the foreword in her book. Within his masterful wordplay, he lays out his thoughts on the text and compares it to The Strange Career of Jim Crow, a book that our late great Martin Luther King Jr. dubbed the civil rights bible. Then, he also challenges the reader to take up the banner of the love of one another and owning social change once they complete the text. From his three pages of text, it is enough to set the reader on fire to want to get into page one and begin the personal journey of change.

"I was thinking of writing a little foreword saying that history is, after all, based on people's recollections, which change with time. -Frederik Pohl

# CHAPTER 10

Introduction

Chapter 10: Introduction

When it comes to the introduction of a book, in my mind, I see it like an M.C. on stage with a mic bringing out the starring act of the night. In the introduction, another writer, or the author himself, introduces you to the topic you are about to read about in the book. They may give you an overall snapshot of the subject matter and give you some inside perspective on why they decided to write the matter. In some introductions, they may give you a detailed layout about how to read their book, what sections contain what, the processes they went through while writing the project, etc. When you formally define a book's introduction, you find that this text, essentially a short chapter, is meant to provide information on what the book will be about. It gives background information, discusses why the book is essential, and gives an overview of the contents.

In the section above, I spoke about my mindset when writing forewords for people. Writing intros can be even more nerve-racking than writing forewords. When penning a foreword, I give my thoughts on the book. In the introduction phase, I am trying to summarize the book somewhat without giving the reader too much. I want to hook their attention and get them on the edge of their seat for what the writer has in store for them. It is like a great pass from Chris Paul. You just want to put the big man in a position to score and let them do the rest. I am telling you these inside thoughts because I like the future writers and consumers of books to understand the various pockets of thinking we have to go into depending on what we are writing at the time. Writing is like sports when you are playing ball under different circumstances. Writing for myself is like playing streetball with no referee, calling your fouls, nobody calling plays, etc. Writing other projects with other people can be like playing with three referees; they are calling every single thing, and you have a T.V. audience eyeballing you all at once. So, you must be aware of what is being asked of you and what your task is for the moment, and then master that particular pocket of writing.

My best example of a great introduction would be the book Lies My Teacher Told

Me, written by James Loewen. In this publication, Loewen gives a detailed thesis of why he felt inspired to write this book after working in the education system for so long, behind the scenes, helping to create the history textbooks that most schools used. He explained why most children struggle to connect with the subject of history in school and what could be done to improve this aspect of education. In the introduction, he also details behind the scenes how some major publishing companies construct their history books and why we rarely see progress in this genre. Lastly, in the introduction, he drills down why American history is essential and how vital it is to teach it precisely as it took place. Not how we would like it to have been.

"Allow me to reintroduce myself /My name is H.O.V."

-Jay Z. Jigga man

# CHAPTER 11
Afterword

Chapter11: Afterword

Nothing puts the cap on a great book like a well written afterward. Most of us know the feeling of reading a good book that you do not want it to end. You have gone all this way, investing your time in this publication, and now you have the last few pages left. The right words will make you close the back cover and lay your head back, trying to digest what you have just read mentally. By definition, an afterword is the portion of a book typically written by a person other than the author. Thank God for me; I have my beautiful mother writing the afterword in this publication. My mother was a librarian before I was born, and I grew up with her having books in almost every inch of the room. So, I could not have a book about reading, and she does not have a part in it somehow. Many times, in the afterword, the writer often tries to do what I call Landing the plane. As a public speaker, if I am asked to be the closing speaker for an event, my mindset is that I am the last person this crowd will see and hear today. I have to say or do something impactful that will stick with them about this event. I feel the same way as a writer. To this point, I have not had the pleasure of writing an afterword for someone, but I will maintain the same mindset when that opportunity does come.

To my future writers, when you sit down to pen an afterword, you want to make sure that you have read the complete work yourself( which I strongly advise for the above parts as well) because, in your afterword, you want to put a nice bow on what the reader has just taken in within the text.

One of my best examples of a powerful afterword would be the book Black Presidency by Dr. Michael Eric Dyson. Within his afterword, he tightly wrapped up how the Obama presidency waned, how it took flight from the beginning, and how it got to where it is currently. He also provided vivid details on their long-standing personal relationship to validate his stance in the text above his afterword. He delivered his glowing compliments and dished out his sharp criticism about the former president within a few pages to drive home his final analysis on a 346-page book. I highly suggest reading any of Dr. Dyson's writings to study any part of the writing process. "Writing is brave. You are Brave."

# OG AFTERWORD

## OG Afterword: Versana Polidore (AKA Mama Vee)

One of my favorite quotes reads, "What I love most about reading is it gives you the ability to reach higher ground and keep climbing. (Oprah Winfrey)

As a lifelong educator, I am thrilled to watch people escape to a world far away that they may never get to visit physically. There is something about reading that feeds you facts about cultures and a deeper understanding of others.

"The more words you know, the more clearly and powerfully you will think. (Wilfred Funk) Knowledge is your superpower. Strive to push your limits. Feed your brain new words and concepts.

Do not be a book skimmer. Digest your books. One activity I enjoy is called Book Tasting. A set of book synopsis is placed around the room, and people read a passage and add book titles to a "to be read" list.

Reading is a no-judgment zone. If you decide after a few chapters that your interest has not peaked, it is okay to continue reading. If you force yourself to finish it, what did you gain from the read if you were not invested in it? You may return to that title another time and see it in a different light.

It is never too late to fine-tune your habits. Grab your highlighters and note cards. Approach your book in a new way. Keep climbing. Your brain will thank you.

# AFTERWORD
Remix

## Afterword Remix: Reggie Bailey, AKA Reggie Reads

When I was a youngin reading Slam by Walter Dean Myers, Bud Not Buddy by Christopher Paul Curtis, Archie Comics, Ramona Quimby, or whatever the book of the time was, I had a simple thought when it came to the so called Anatomy of a Book: There is an author who wanted to create a story so they wrote, and then they made a book, and they sold it—voila, magic. I didn't know or care about publishing companies authors typically sign with to get their books out to the masses. I didn't know or care about the many departments that exist within a publishing house that help get books out to the masses. I didn't know or care about the different imprints that exist within a publishing house. I didn't know about the Big 5 publishing houses (Penguin Random House, HarperCollins, Simon & Schuster, MacMillan & Hachette, which used to be the Big 6 before Penguin & Random House merged). I didn't know about Independent Presses or Self-Published authors. In short, I was ignorant to the business of books, & knew what sections of a book were called more so than understanding the anatomy of a book.

The year 2020 took the world by storm through a global pandemic that kept millions of people in their homes & as of this writing, has cost millions of people their lives. Global protests happened in response to the murders of George Floyd, Breonna Taylor, & Ahmaud Arbery & Donald Trump was still president of the United States.

Those of us who are connoisseurs of dystopian literature—Brave New World, 1984, Fahrenheit 451, Parable of the Sower, The Fifth Season, Chain Gang All-Stars, The Book of Revelations—might have thought we were in the end times. There were also those people who, in these end times, knew that there were still stories to tell—lessons that needed to be taught, anatomies that needed to be understood. Seanathan Polidore happened to be one of those people.

In October of 2020, I was uniquely creating content—doing Instagram Lives every Sunday as one half a dynamic duo that would go on to become Books Are Pop Culture—but Sean was publishing The

Anatomy of a Book, which happened to be his 5th book published overall & his 4th book published in 2020 alone. That's right, in 2020, Sean published four books giving his favorite mixtape rappers from the days of Dat Piff & Gangsta Grillz a run for their money.

Sean, a lifelong reader & book enthusiast, knew another harsh truth about end times & took advantage: when disaster strikes opportunity arises. During the COVID-19 Pandemic there were people losing their lives and getting sick in a way that would alter their lives & there were also people who used this time—a time with less people out & about moving through the world, a spike in unemployment—to bring a level of production to their passion that might have seemed unthinkable in our pre-pandemic world. Sean poured into his passion for books and literature by self-publishing four titles within a 5-month span during the summer and fall of 2020. The Anatomy of a Book was his fourth & final publication after The Butterfly Effect, The 5 Laws of Leadership & The Hero's Journey, respectively.

In The Anatomy of a Book Sean spends the first part of the book giving sound advice on how & why to read alongside the benefits of reading. In the second part he gets into the eponymous anatomy by letting readers know why you shouldn't skip over sections like the introduction, about the author, the Afterword (which, in this case especially, I'll need you to read). The Anatomy of a Book is, therefore, quite literally, a book about books, a book about reading, a love letter to books, knowledge, & words, the encouragement that readers of all ages have been looking for in a bite-sized chunk.

The bit about this being a bite-sized chunk is significant because Sean has often talked about—like so many who remember the world before the extended hand (our smartphones) in recent years—the crisis of our attention, the distractions getting out of hand, adjusting your content so that it stands out in a world dominated by reels, 280 characters or less statements, memes, TikTok videos & YouTube Shorts. With What's Your Kick? Sean's debut, which he published in 2017. He wrote a 140-page book, but his 4 books from 2020 total out to 147 pages. Sean saw short-form content becoming the dominant form of consumption & decided to adapt his literature accordingly. With books like Anatomy of a Book, expert readers can affirm existing knowledge of how books work & new readers can inch quickly towards the level of expertise in less than an hour's time.

A lot of times, when we speak about addiction, we think about it in a negative light. The things we reach a level of not being able to live without distract us from our work & our passions, but with The Anatomy of a Book and Sean's catalog in general, he is tempting readers, mostly in bite-sized chunks, with the addiction of literature. Now that you've made it to these words—the end times within this text—I'll say this: Welcome to the best addiction there is. The bite-sized chunk is a great place to start; now, go cook yourself some meals, even meal prep, if you feel inclined. As Sean would even tell you, literature is the best way to get full.

# AN ODE TO READING

## An Ode to Reading: Tamika Rasheed

I deliver you the world. Shaped and modeled like poetry, I give your life. Despite tales of the lost and lonely, you will receive peace. Thus, with every word crafted for a prosperous future, like a mother carrying her newborn child, I give you books.

My future, without any chance, was written for me. Bound by the confines of bricks and statistics used as a form of oppression, I was never to make it out. However, through pure determination and profound hope, I changed the course of my life with straightforward action. I found the library.

So, like a beacon at night, the library housed a safe place for me. I did not know that walking through those library doors on the first day was like a key to a world that I was told could never be within my reach because I was a black girl from the projects.

I was captivated. Taken like the moon does the sea, that single place held the many nuances of life. I found myself discovering worlds, being accepted by clubs, and solving mysteries, and it was all through books housed in this sacred place.

Each time I walked through those doors, I educated myself through books. Each time I entered those walls, it was like an uncharted path that led me to my dreams. So, unbeknownst to me, I became uplifted and dared to dream of bigger things.

I began to realize that I found salvation through books. So, I wondered how many in the world didn't even know that readers could save lives. Given the opportunity, how many others would learn to love books and utilize them as a safe haven?

With that said, I took to arms and decided to educate. I wanted to give back to this world what was so freely given to me, and the only way I knew to do that was through books.

Books saved my life. They gave me the courage to thrive, even when I did not feel like thriving. They gave me meaning when the world showed its ugly face, and books made the world a safe place.

Points to Consider

1. What colors do you find work best for you to highlight? What is your favorite method to make things stick to your mind? Is it underlining, highlighting, note-taking, or recording yourself?

2. Where is your perfect place to read? What is your home's most comfortable, relaxed, quiet, and best-lit place? Is it best for you to read and study outside your home? Do you need a physical book or read better with an eBook?

3. When it comes to travel, name some places you would love to visit. Now, go on your smartphone or computer and search for some books on the topic. What would you imagine doing in those places? Would you imagine just visiting this place, or would you want to relocate there for good?

4. What is your current relationship with words? Do you love comments? Do you care about the words that you say? Do you care how you sound when you try to communicate your feelings and thoughts? What are some methods you can use to help you increase your vocabulary? Who is your favorite rapper, writer, or poet, and what is their vocabulary? Have you ever wanted to learn a different language? If so, which one would it be?

5. How do you think your educational performance would be if you were to read more books? What specific class would you like to bring your grades up in?

6. When you read your books, how often do you read ALL of the books? Do the various parts of the text displayed in this publication usually interest you before having a detailed explanation of what their purpose serves here? Do you see yourself possibly considering these sections in your future readings?

7. What aspects of your history are you curious about? What parts of the account do you feel would benefit you the most from investigating? How much of your history do you think you have gained in your school thus far?

Reading Tip: Check the Footage

For most of the books I decide to read, I make a point to YouTube and the author before I get the book. Most times, you will find footage of the writer in an interview about the book, a book signing, or on their promo tour leading up to the release date. During these clips, you can get a great handle on the research they did leading up to writing the book, why they decided to write on the topic, what difficulty they faced along the way, and some hidden facts you may not find within the book itself. Another added value I have seen in doing this is that as you read the book, you can almost hear the author's voice in your head as if he is laying it out for you. Even if you cannot find footage on that particular book, you have decided to read it, and you may still be able to find some video on the writer. You can still gauge how they think, speak, put words together, function, and expectations, which can still be a bonus for you as a reader. This is another excellent speed-reading tip because the more you know about a subject before you read it, the quicker you can get through the content because you have a base of knowledge about it. Something unfamiliar to you will naturally take longer to go through because you are trying to wrap your mind around the content. Watching videos and getting background knowledge on the topic or the author before you tackle the book is a great way to read it faster and increase your enjoyment of the book as you connect the dots between the footage and the words on the page. Happy reading!

Sean P.

Recommended Reading List:

How to Improve Your Memory and Remember Anything

How to Read a Book

How to Speed Read

Mind Mapping for Writers

Morning Rituals Ultimate Methods

The Power of Concentration

The Power of Now

Success Through Stillness

10 Days to Faster Reading

As a Man Thinketh

# The Butterfly Effect

by: Seanathan Polidore, MSP

**Table of Contest:**

Foreword: Kofi Piesie……………….…101

Remixed Introduction: Dr. Ashley Wade……………………………………106

 OG Introduction: Anthony Bey………....109

Phase 1: Starting Ugly (Who wants to be a caterpillar?)…………………………….....112

Phase 2: Embrace the Darkside (Cocoon)…………………………………...115

Phase 3: Only YOU Can Save You (Breaking Point)……………………………………119

Phase 5: Overview……………………122

Afterword: LeKesha Ingram, MSW,ASW…………………………....125

# FOREWORD

Foreword: Kofi Piesie

Out of Chaos comes **ORDER, HARMONY, ORGANIZATIONAL,** AND **PEACE.** We are just like the Caterpillar where the Gardner knows it is beneficial, so does the Universe know we are beneficial. Caterpillars metamorphose into butterflies or moths (Lepidoptera), and caterpillars become important pollinators for many different plants. Through Chaos or dark times, we metamorphose into something that can be beneficial or harmful, and that comes with what decision you make to **CHANGE** your dark and Chaotic State.

Caterpillars turn into butterflies. Some turn into moths instead. No matter what, all caterpillars go through the same four stages: egg, larva, pupa, and adult. Each stage has different **goals** and **time lengths**. Let us return to the moment I mentioned that a Caterpillar becomes an important pollinator. Now, some of you may be asking, what is a pollinator? A pollinator is anything that helps carry pollen from the male part of the flower (stamen) to the female part of the same or another flower (stigma). The movement of pollen must occur for the plant to become fertilized and produce fruits, seeds, and young plants. Some plants are self-pollinating, while others may be fertilized by pollen carried by wind or water. Still, other flowers are pollinated by insects and animals - such as bees, wasps, moths, butterflies, birds, flies, and small mammals, including bats.

A pollinator is necessary for our food through change from the caterpillar into the butterfly. Yes, that's right. One out of every three bites of food you eat exists because of the efforts of pollinators. Healthy ecosystems depend on pollinators. Insects and animals pollinate at least 75 percent of all the flowering plants on earth.

**Change** details many things; like one may change bad eating habits to live, and those changes change his or her life for the better and his or her family. Sometimes, bad things are drawn to us to change the ripples of life in a better direction. Sometimes, the ripples of life put us in bad places where we feel stuck or sinking in quicksand. Most People want a better life for themselves and the ones they care for but are scared to make changes they need in order to get that life, complaining about a better relationship with their significant other, more money, a better career, or owning their own business is not going get them any of those things.

You must be willing to transform and make the changes needed to metamorphose into the thing you need to change your ripples of life into the very thing you want and desire to do.

Become like those pollinators or, my new term, a "**changenator**." Make changes that will better your life and everyone else around you. Carry your goals, ideals, and dreams from your mind and materialize them into real things you can see and touch. Don't let adversity change your vision; change your strategy and approach. By staying patient and being consistent, it will pay off/payout.

Before I end this foreword, I would like to share a personal story about myself in a place of darkness and chaos. As a young man, I made some not-so-smart decisions that led me behind bars for some time. With those not-so-smart decisions, I lost my car, my girl, my money, and my job. I was caged like an animal, and you could say I was being domesticated. That was 22 years ago, and I have metamorphosed from a caterpillar into a blossoming butterfly that is beneficial to my family, friends, and community. The changes I made in my everyday decision-making and how I never let rough times make me make wrong decisions that would cause harm to myself and possibly to others around me. Don't be afraid to change for the better. A small change can turn into a bigger and better change, which will add value and happiness to your life.

I hope you enjoyed this section of the book, and now you are ready for the meat and potatoes of this book, where Seanathan Polidore shares with us the Butterfly Effect and its impact on our lives.

# INTRODUCTION REMIX

Introduction Remix: Dr Ashley Wade

The Butterfly Effect

This process won't waste your time. Just in case you were wondering. I understand why we would think life's processes would. Because life is complicated, the responsibilities, the expectations, and the encounters- without proper understanding- can leave one confused, doubtful, and low vibrational. We see a lot of this around us. The regularity, the mundane, has caused unhappiness within people across the world and oftentimes leaving people dependent on pharmaceuticals for functional mental health.
We lose the motivation to meet challenges head-on because somewhere in our experience, one has perceived that life has gotten the best of them, but I want us to add this thought to our process. The creator is on our side. Yes. I read the following quote in the Kolbrin Bible, and it changed my life, "No life is without conflict." I interpreted that as this message: since conflict will come, then processing, understanding, and elevation are necessary tools to build into

that genuine self-esteem, worth, and personal value. We must capture the lessons and values that come with this experience and be willing to walk in new form. We view the hard lessons as undesirable, so we learn not to welcome the changes that are inevitable. We have all been miseducated into the perfection mindset without realizing that the process is important, revelations are important, and development is important. It's time to re-educate us and decipher life with intention so that once the butterfly is revealed, it can live out its beauty meaningfully, radiantly, and to the fullest. Allow openness and creativity to change the Universe.

Continue to Seek and Be Light, So You Can Be You and Max That Shit Out!

Dr. Ashley Wade

# OG
# INTRODUCTION

OG Introduction: Anthony Bey

In Chaos Theory, the "Butterfly Effect" is the sensitive dependence on initial conditions in which a slight change in one state of a deterministic nonlinear system can result in significant differences in a later state. Put it means that a small change can make a much more substantial change happen, OR it can be summed up and the Law of Cause and Effect.

The "Butterfly Effect" concept has been around since the beginning of creation and has probably been used by you without realizing it. Applying a small change that produces a more noticeable and perhaps better difference or result has been used in communities, politics, education, diets, religion, rehabilitation centers, personal life, the workforce, etc. A few examples are when a person changes and implements behavior that produces a bigger and better change in results in the outcome of their life: the power of prayer, social distancing, wearing a seat belt, a change in thought pattern, administrative changes, the taking of medications, and the hero's journey to name a few. In each of the examples, the change begins with a thought, takes a split second to occur, and can only happen in the darkness of the mind. Then, once the change application happens, it must be observed and practiced consistently. Depending on the situation and desired outcome, some applied changes may take longer to manifest than others, but if one will but DECIDE to change and COMMIT, they will surely SUCCEED. Throughout this reading, it is intended that a few things become apparent; change happens in the mind; first, separation from the old has to happen, consistency of action is critical, and success is eventual but can only be defined by YOU. The learning will increase as the desire to change grows more robust and the actual work to change is done.

YOU MUST PUT IN THE WORK!

# PHASE 1
Starting Ugly

Phase 1: Starting Ugly

For change to occur in our lives, be it fitness, business, or relationships, we must have a clearly defined starting point for our journey. Just like on our GPS in the car, we have a red dot (the destination) and a blue dot (the starting location); the same goes when trying to reach our dreams in life. One of the main things that holds people back from their goals from the onset is that they want to START pretty! They want to begin on day one and perform as well as others who may have been in that particular industry for years. This is a great way to set yourself up for disappointment and failure time and time again. It would not be the best idea to join a gym today and crave to have the body of a CrossFit athlete immediately. You do not want to sit across from the financial guru to improve your situation and lie about your incoming debts instead of exposing the ugly truths that landed you in their office. Only having the ability to have an honest assessment of where you are currently will put you on the right track to your overall goals in the end. Make no mistake, It takes a lot of heart and courage to start ugly. The road to true transformation is not for the faint of heart, but for those who endure, the triumph is sweet. Of all my years observing tattoos, I have seen tons of people with beautiful butterfly tattoos, but I have never seen a person say, "hey, give me the slithery, slimy, oozing, nasty caterpillar right on my lower back." Because nobody wants to embrace and embody such a creature in their creative expressions, we want to be beautiful and majestic in our pursuits, but we must realize that the ugly part is the vehicle we must use to take flight.

"We all want to be fly, but nobody wants to be the caterpillar"- Sean P.

# PHASE 2

Embrace the Dark Side (Cocoon)

## Phase 2: Embrace the Dark Side (Cocoon)

From most major religions to movies, books, and fables, we are all given this fear in our subconscious of things that bump into the night. Almost everything you could think of regarding dark or black has a negative connotation. Think of Black magic, Black holes, Black cats. In the Star Wars film, evil is represented by the Dark Side, and the most iconic villain ever wore all Black. So, it is effortless to understand why, in life, one of the main things we would want to avoid is putting ourselves into the preverbal darkness. Now, let us change our focus for a brief moment to some of the great things that we gain from the darkness. Let us consider the creation story for a moment. It does not matter if you believe in God saying, "Let there be light," the Big Bang theory, or another school of thought; the one thing we can agree on is before the beginning, all was in triple darkness, then the birth of planets, stars, moons, and suns, etc. Let us flip the script for a moment to the female body. She carries the baby inside her dark womb for the nine-month gestation period and then gives birth to the fantastic baby that brings light to the family around it. In the case of the caterpillar, it has to cut itself off from the security of the ground that it knows so well and make itself vulnerable, perched up high above the earth for all predators to see. He has to go to a closed-in and cut-off place to be still and have the rebirth he is designed for! Some of us are running from the very things meant to shape and mold us because we are afraid to be cut off from our comfort zones. We love to be plugged into social media night and day. We cannot wait to get around our coworkers and friends to have a voice to hear outside of our own. We rely on relationships repeatedly, even if they are false ones, to help us identify who we are in the world. We must learn the art of getting truly comfortable enough with ourselves that we can afford to unplug from the outside world and tap into the deepest parts of ourselves. This COVID-19 epidemic has revealed a lot to us all. Unfortunately, we were forced to "shut down" for months at a time, and we had to leave the jobs we spent over forty hours a week in and the extra activities we drown ourselves in to escape that world. Very quickly, we saw the depression, anxiety, and other mental health ills spike as people were made to face themselves in a thoughtful way they may have never before. Some people were able to take this time and learn new skills, renovate their spaces, and change their bodies. Isolation can be painful to some and revealing to others. Some of the most outstanding leaders this world has ever birthed came from times of forced isolation. Malcolm X, Huey P. Newton, and Mandela were all transformed and forged in dark places that were extremely uncomfortable and unbearable conditions. I am not saying it takes a world pandemic or hard prison time to elevate ourselves. Still, we should take periods to ourselves when we shut ourselves off from the world, and we work on taking a long, hard look at our circumstances and thinking of ways to emerge from our darkness better and brighter than before when we emerged to the world.

"You cannot defeat me with the Dark. I was born in the Dark, and I was made in the Dark and thrived in the Dark!"-Bane, Batman Dark Knight.

# PHASE 3

The Breaking Point

Phase 3: The Breaking Point

The most important part about the caterpillar-to-butterfly process that most people miss is how important it is for the butterfly to break free from the bondage of the cocoon. A mentor once told this beautiful story about this process. In hindsight, I don't know if this tale holds scientifically or is a case of a complete fable, but the principle holds just the same. You see, if you walk by a cocoon hanging there and you feel as if you are doing the butterfly a favor by cracking him out of the cocoon, you will kill him because he will not have enough strength in his wings to take flight and feed himself nor protect himself from predators. When the caterpillar is inside the chrysalis, it pumps and flexes its wings during the transformation process. He is building strength in his wings against the outer shell of the cocoon. It is like he is in there doing push-ups, getting bigger and more vital to face this world.

The change comes from resistance, like going to the gym with a workout partner. You may use a spotter for safety reasons, but if you know anything about the science of working out, the last thing you want is your partner taking the weight from you. You know your body shapes and firms up under resistance, just like going to the gym with a workout partner. You may use a spotter for safety reasons, but if you know anything about the science of working out, the last thing you want is your partner taking the weight from you. You know your body shapes and firms up under the resistance of the weight. We must learn to resist the urge to look for someone or something on the outside of us to save us in times of great despair. We may be in the perfect place to build up into the person you need to be to get those big goals you have planned for yourself.

# OVERVIEW

Overview

In closing, we all have the power to transform our lives from our current conditions if we genuinely want to. It all starts with a critical observation of yourself and admitting to yourself just where you are in the process right now. Embrace where you are and be in a mindset of hope, knowing that most of the rags-to-riches stories we all idolize started where you are, if not worse. Next, we learn that a vital stage in the transformation process will be isolating yourself from the outside noise and distractions of life to hear your inner voice. There are countless accounts of great leaders who had to endure their time of darkness and being alone. Some of the beautiful things we admire in the brightest lights came out of the incubator of darkness. Lastly, we must learn the mindset we all must do for ourselves. No one is coming to save you, and even if they could, it would do more harm than good to your overall mission in life. The strength that we gain and the belief in ourselves overcoming the most formidable odds give us the courage to take on our biggest goals with the confidence that we can survive what this life can throw at us.

# AFTERWORD

## Afterword: Lekesha Ingram, MSW, ASW

Dear Reader,
Congratulations! You have just finished reading an amazing book that will have a lasting impact on your life. Getting out of your comfort zone is no easy feat. It requires courage, determination, and a willingness to confront the unknown. It is a journey that can be both exciting and frightening as you push the boundaries of what you thought was ever possible. Throughout this book, Seanathan has offered invaluable tools and insights to help you navigate the path ahead and the challenges that will most assuredly arise when stepping outside your comfort zone. However, dear Reader, it is crucial not to forget that this is where growth often occurs, outside the boundaries of comfort. Embrace the discomfort, for it is a sign that you are growing. Embrace the challenges, for they are opportunities in disguise. And most importantly, embrace yourself, for you are capable of achieving greatness beyond your wildest imagination. May the lessons within these pages stay with you, guiding you through every step of your journey. Remember, you have the power to shape

your own destiny. So, go forth confidently, embrace the unknown, and fearlessly pursue your dreams. Wishing you a life filled with extraordinary adventures and the fulfillment of all your aspirations.
With warmest regards,
 Kesha Ingram (@bookishblackgirl)

Points to Consider

In this section of the book, just as I did in What's Your Kick, I want to give you the space and opportunity to make this book yours by asking thoughtful questions for you to ponder.

1. What areas in your life haven't been willing to start as ugly as you should?

2. If you could picture yourself as the complete butterfly, what would that look, feel, smell, sound like to you?

3. What darkness have you been running from for so long in your life?

4. On a scale of 1 through 5, 5 being the most favorable, how would you rate your level of comfort in isolation from the distractions of the outside world?

5. In times of adversity and resistance, do you tend to look for others to take the weight from you, or do you lean on being more self-reliant?

6. List three people you may have in your circle that could help you hold up a true mirror to yourself to aid in your self-assessment process.

# The Five Laws of Leadership

by Seanathan Polidore, MSP

**Table of Contents:**

Acknowledgments............................132

Dedication......................................134

Foreword: Origin Story....................135

Foreword Remix: Kofi Piese..............137

Introduction: By AnthonyBell.............145

Introduction Remix: Dr. Ashley Wade..........................................149

Law 1: Leadership Starts with Yourself (The Inside Job).......................................153

Law 2: Keep Your Intent on Serving Others (How may I help you?).....................157

Law 3: Don't Be A Leader for Likes (Do anything forClout)............................161

Law 4: Take the Initiative (Go Getter, Go Getter)........................................165

Law 5: Be A Trendsetter (Make Your Wave)..........................................170

Afterword: Raymond Dockery III..........176

Acknowledgments:

I would love to start my thanks with the readers! That's right. You are the ones that keep me going and keep my fire lit when it comes to doing these projects. Without you supporting my efforts and giving me feedback, I would be writing to myself, which is called journaling. I want to thank my family for always helping me and making me feel confident that I can do anything I set out to do so I can operate in the boldest manner possible. I have to give a special shout-out to my business partner and brother, Cliff Roy Jr., for helping me in so many ways behind the scenes, in front of the scenes, and on top of the scenes. I cannot thank you enough for opening up so many things I could not have done alone. I want to thank my mentor and guide, Anthony Bell, for always directing me and sparking me up for these missions. I want to give a special shout-out to my wonderful mother. I am always the first to jump up and go beyond the call to make sure I have all the intellectual material I could dream of and the first to spread the word from the top of the mountain. Lastly, I thank my big brother Doc for contributing to this book. He was the first person I met to show me the power of written words through his writing ability and his command of the English language. Without him knowing it, he was sparking something inside me that had been set ablaze ever since. Without him, there would be no books.

Dedication:

This book is dedicated to my grandparents. The late Mrs. Dora Jean Lewis and Mr. Cornelius Lewis Jr. are Two of the finest examples of Leadership I saw with my own two eyes. I live to make you proud.

# FOREWORD

## Foreword: Origin Story

Four years ago, I was asked by a youth organization for leaders to give a presentation to the group on the topic of leading. I went to work right away, picking my brain on the fundamental principles that I felt every leader needed to cultivate in all areas of Leadership, be it school, business, military, or sport. Over the years, I have done this speech countless times for various schools, sports teams, and other organizations. The pages you are about to read are an extension of my notes, slides, and thoughts from that presentation brought to paper for the first time. These short novellas are meant to be universal, but I have my younger readers in mind as I write this because they are the world's future leaders. Yes, there are a million Leadership books on the shelf to dig into, but what will set this apart will be how much I intend to communicate the application portions of this book. The more you interact with this publication and not just passively turn pages, the more you will be able to forge into the type of leader you dreamed of being.

# FOREWORD REMIX

## Foreword Remix: Kofi Piesie

I am always looking at the past and studying our great leaders who are now Ancestors. Men like Alexander Crummell, W.E.B Du Bois, Paul Dunbar, Carter G Woodson, Arturo Alfonso Schomburg, and many other great men who were part of The American Negro Academy during this time in the late 19th Century and early 20$^{th}$ Century. They began to develop this philosophy, The Talent Tenth, which was an essay W.E.B Du Bois wrote and published in 1903.

Talented Tenth is a term that designated a leadership class of African Americans in the early 20th century. Although the term was created by white Northern philanthropists, it is primarily associated with W. E. B. Du Bois. The "Talented Tenth" refers to the one in ten Black men who have cultivated the ability to become leaders of the Black community by acquiring a college education, writing books, and becoming directly involved in social change.

**What is leadership?**

Leadership is the ability of an individual or a group of people to influence and guide followers or members of an organization, society, or team. Leadership is often an attribute tied to a person's title, seniority, or ranking in a hierarchy. However, it's an attribute anyone can have or attain, even those without leadership positions. It's a developable skill that can be improved over time.

Back to the men in American Negro Academy. They had this each one teach one mentality where they would teach, guide, and set the right example for the people in their communities. They would lead in a way that would help their community improve and excel to greater heights, which would also birth more leaders in the process.

**What are some characteristics of a leader?**

- Self-Awareness
- Respect
- Compassion
- Vision
- Communication
- Learning Agility

- Collaboration
- Influence
- Integrity
- Courage
- Gratitude
- Resilience
- Hardworking
- Understanding
- Bold
- Great Listener
- Servant
- Good Character

Some may ask what qualifies you or the author to write about leadership and being a leader. Ok, no sweat, I gotcha. I have worked quite a few jobs, and in most of them, I have been promoted to Team Lead, Supervisor, or Manager. In those jobs, I was promoted to lead a department, exceed all goals, and groom the next up-and-coming leader for the department. I also work for a company where I lead a class of supervisors, where every quarter, I would teach and reteach how to lead and how to be professional. I am also a Free Mason, and I was a head officer called the W.M. I led a group of black men for 5 years with my vision to help them become better men and help the communities that needed help. Within the Masonic organization, we had a youth program called the Trail Master, in which I led a group of young boys from 12 to 18 years of age. I can keep going, but I will digress now because this book is not about me. I just wanted to share some leading roles I was involved in.

The Author of the book is also qualified to speak about leadership. Senathan Poildore, first and foremost, is a leader of his household; he and his wife set the standard, govern, and set laws for the home. Seanathan Polidore is a former Professor at the University of Lafayette and SLCC. He Led, guided, and taught the next generation. Seanathan was also a leader in his practice of counseling and a leader in the fitness world, where he trained young children and adults.

**What is Laws?**

Oxford Dictionary states: 1. LAWS is the system of rules which a particular country or community recognizes as regulating the actions of its members and which it may enforce by the imposition of penalties. 2. a rule defining correct procedure or behavior in a sport.

Okay, so now you have an understanding of what a law or laws are. Seanathan Polidore lays out in this book his 5 laws for leadership.

7. Law 1 - Leadership Starts with Yourself… The Inside Job
8. Law 2- Keep Your Intent of Serving Other..how may I help you?)
9. Law-3 Don't Be A Leader for Likes.. Do Anything for Clout
10. Law 4- Take the initiative… Go Getter, Go Getter
11. Law 5- Be Trendsetter…Make Your Own Wave

Each law in each chapter gives you the correct procedure on what to do and how to cultivate leadership qualities from within and out. There are many characteristics that make a good leader, but, in my opinion, serving and helping others are the most vital ones. When looking through the historical records of our great leaders of the past, like Martin Luther King, Marcus Garvey,

Malcolm X, Kwame Ture, and Fannie Lou Hamer, they were helping the people from state to state and in other countries. They were servants for the people.

I mention good character early, and this is where outstanding leadership comes in. One must possess this quality. This would be my second most vital quality or characteristic of a good leader. I read an article a few years ago about character, and the author of that published article says something along the lines of good character is one's habits, actions, and emotional responses all are united and directed toward the moral and the good. I love that, so if you are morally rich, then each law that is spoken about and each quality of a leader will not be a problem for becoming a great leader, mentor, and great example for birthing more leaders.

## My Conclusion

In conclusion, I wanted to culminate and emphasize the critical role of character in leadership. Good character encompasses habits, actions, and emotional responses directed toward good morals, which is essential for a leader. This character forms the foundation upon which the laws of leadership are built, enabling individuals to become effective leaders and mentors and inspiring the emergence of new leaders. In essence, this book will encourage readers to internalize these laws and qualities to cultivate their leadership potential, thereby making a positive impact in their communities and beyond.

# INTRODUCTION

## Introduction: Anthony Bell

What is a law, and what is leadership? It is a question of context.\ In layman's terms, a law is a governing principle, and Leadership guides a person or people to achieve a common goal. They are two of the most critical aspects of the success of any measure. Without the guiding principles of law and Leadership, a person, group, or organization will surely soon meet its demise with reckless abandon. However, one aspect of direction and Leadership that is overlooked is the "spiritual" aspect, which is the cornerstone of "ALL LAW." To be a great leader, one must have solid spiritual fortitude and a sound mind, providing excellent results as some decisions are tough to make and may require a battle with oneself. Do not get "the spiritual" confused with "the religious," as they are genuinely not related, and by no means is this statement meant to offend.

The essence of law is universal and internal; therefore, based on the knowledge thereof, a person acts, behaves, projects, and exudes accordingly. The guiding laws of righteousness, moral rectitude, compassion, strength, etc., are written in your DNA…however, they must be acknowledged and practiced to be fully effective. We know right from wrong, truth from falsehood, and sound from evil. Consider "The Laws of Leadership" the yin and yang of your new experiences of endeavor. When applied right, you, the lawful leader, shine as a beacon of light in your organization or business and a community pillar.

There is a formula to your success, and only YOU can solve it, but first, you must have the foundation: Knowledge, Wisdom, and Understanding. These three refining guidelines are precursors to anything you may want to achieve. You must know by reading, become wise, and gain experience through doing. Finally, you must demonstrate your understanding by showing your work. There is no shortcut to success, and those who take that road will get cut short. Immense success is not guaranteed for all, but your success is inevitable for those guided by doing great business and solving problems. As you read the chapters ahead, allow your mind to envision what you want, let your heart desire it, and do the work to bring into existence your success.

# INTRODUCTION REMIX

## Introduction Remix: Dr. Ashley Wade

Great people,
Welcome to the next level of your journey in the exploration of Leadership. Let me start by saying that one of the things I enjoy the most about Sean is his ability to teach. This book is an incredible testament to that, and I encourage you to read all of his books. He took a broad concept like leadership and broke it down into the 5 most important laws for Leadership. These 5 Laws of Leadership are completely tangible and applicable in your Journey of Personal and Professional Development. I like that these Laws are about philosophy, not a quick psychological scheme. Leadership is deeper than any single ability; it's more about utilizing and oscillating through your natural tools and abilities while continuously adding to your psyche. It's a concept that you have to be open to embodying that requires willingness, execution… and a little razzle. Realize the things that make You Unique (that's your razzle) and elevate those gifts, take the steps to evolve and contribute to your character building along the way. This book is a tool to help you see Yourself in a different light

regarding Leadership and Your Place in the Movement. WE need each other to be Activated, Aware, and Operating in our Highness as much as possible on a regular basis in this World. Yes, you'll see that it is a Personal and Spiritual experience because as you explore through self-discovery, there will be supernatural communication via signs and signals that lead you to the illumination of your path. Most people say they believe this but remain stuck because they don't trust it. It's all in what you Believe. We only expect the tangibles of success to reach everyone else without realizing that you can Activate the Leader inside of You, tipping your domino effect. Also, I would like to address the fact that we have been shown a narrow lens of what leadership looks like. This is strategic. I encourage you to look at Leadership beyond face value and Accept that You have What it Takes! Take The 5 Laws of Leadership and use them as a launching pad and Ignite the Powers you possess in This phase of your journey. Pay attention because as you include these into your habits, the Universe will respond with Elevation. Lastly, I encourage you to continue Reading. I've found that my favorite Leaders are not taught

about the traditional education system, so add these phenomenal Leaders to your research: Ella Baker, Fannie Lou Hamer, and Elaine Brown. Find yourself Inspired and Remember to Maximize the Experience of Your Life.
Ase'.
Dr. Ashley Wade
-Pharmacist, Author, Curator, Literacy and Community Advocate, Griotte.

# LAW 1

Leadership Starts with Yourself

(The Inside Job)

Law 1: Leadership Starts with Yourself (The Inside Job)

Leading others start with how well you command yourself. Oddly enough, most times in life, we find it easier to offer other suggestions and excellent advice, but when it comes to governing ourselves, we fall short time and time again. When you step into a leadership position, you must remember that you are about to be under the most giant microscope you have ever faced because when you put yourself front and center, everyone is watching you. Do you ever notice that during a political season, in the beginning, you may have some candidates you have never heard of before in your life? As the days and weeks press on, the media has uncovered this person's school history, criminal background, spouse's history, parent's dealings, church affiliations, etc. Indeed, for most readers seeing this book, you probably do not plan on running for office, so take a pause and wipe your forehead. (Geesh, that was close) But there will still be expectations from you because people want to see their leaders prove that they have been successful at leading themselves up to this point. They will look at your dress style and physical appearance more than usual. Whoever said you could not judge a book by its cover, I don't know what they were thinking. It is sad and judgmental, but it is the world's way. Everyone judges, even if only on a subconscious level. People will watch how you interact with the people superior to you and, more importantly, how you treat the people beneath you to gauge your character.

You must take a profound journey of self-discovery before going into leading others. Take the proper time to learn what drives you and motivates you. Better understand what your personality and character strengths and weaknesses are. More importantly, learn how these attributes impact those around you positively or negatively. Ask yourself how well you take instruction from others and what is the best form of Leadership you like to operate within. The answer to these questions and many more will help shape and mold the leader you will become. You will have to sharpen your daily discipline habits and self-control. The more you display control over yourself, the easier it will be to demand a tight ship from those under you.

Remember, you lead from the inside out. As you command and direct yourself, your ability to make judgment calls on behalf of others will be more effortless.

"If there is no enemy within, the enemy without cannot harm." -African proverb.

# LAW 2

Keep Your Intent on Serving Others

(How may I help you?)

Law 2: Keep Your Intent on Serving Others (How may I help you?)

Being a servant to others should always be in the front of your mind when you decide to step into the shoes of Leadership. Taking on Leadership is one of the most selfless acts you can take. I mention this in more detail later in the publication, but when you are the leader, you must willing take on every situation's good, dire, and ugly. Some people see Leadership as a hey, look at me type of moment, but the most outstanding leaders are the best servants to others, and they accept Leadership from others at a higher level than most. Yes, that's right. When you are in a leadership position, you will still need to have the ability to take instruction and direction from others yourself. The more you are willing to take in Leadership from others, the better leader you can be yourself because you will know what type of Leadership you don't operate under well. Hopefully, that will translate into how you reign over others.

Hospitality… is not just for restaurants and hotels.

Hospitality speaks to how you treat your classmates, teammates, and coworkers. Above all else, hospitality speaks to how you treat absolute strangers. Once again, when you are in the front, all eyes will be on you, and they will observe how you treat others in all senses of the word. How well will you treat someone who cannot do anything for you? How will you respond to an open enemy to your cause? How will you respond when your superiors come into your space? You have to have the ability to put yourself into the shoes of others at all times to make critical decisions that will ripple well beyond you. There are various styles of Leadership, and you will have to decide your way, but I will tell you that the more you can make your team feel empowered and involved in the process, the more it will increase their confidence in themselves, and this will ramp up productivity for your cause.

The best leaders make others around them great. There are tons of players in the Hall of Fame right now, not because their game was so good, but because they were blessed to play alongside a fantastic leader who MADE THEM look like a million bucks. As I mentioned, the best leaders increase those around them, not belittle or diminish them. Remember, the larger the goal, the more you will need strong people in your circle to help with the heavy lifting. It is tough to shoulder every single aspect of a project by yourself. In a little moment, even if you could pull it off alone, try to involve someone and help them feel as if you could not have done it without them. This will be like putting away money for a rainy day down the line when you seriously need it for a more critical matter. You are as strong as your weakest link. It would be in your best interest to take the time and effort to invest a little more in the people that you observe to be lacking in certain areas of your team. Ask yourself, how strongly do you want to be? Whatever that answer is, put it into YOUR team.

"Walk around like a King but do the work of a servant"-Dame Dollar.

# LAW 3

Don't Be a Leader for Likes

(Do anything for Clout)

Law 3: Don't Be a Leader for Likes (Do anything for Clout)

Most great leaders had no idea how big and significant their views would be when they were doing it. They just kept their head down and did the groundwork that was needed by them at the moment. When I think of Martin Luther King Jr, Malcolm X, and Nat Turner and their heroic feats, this was before social media (yes, try to imagine that). This was before "going live," before tweeting, no snapping. They put their actual lives on the line and did something beyond the normal scope of human-type things when they did not know if anybody would ever know about what they were doing. Most of these leaders were not well-liked at the time of their death. They were leaders from a very pure place, and they wanted to make a change in their communities and ultimately impact the world. When some of these heroes died, they were not liked very much by their community and the areas they fought so hard to defend. They lead no matter what. You should not be a leader because it looks excellent on your timeline.

You should not just appear in a place where you know there will be cameras and attention. This goes back to the previous law of your intent when you step up and take charge, to begin with. Trust me, the watch comes and goes in the blink of an eye these days, and if you are thriving high off of today's praise, the harsh comments tomorrow will cripple you. In this microwave society, the next big thing in the news will happen in 30 seconds or less. Lead for the people or stay on the sidelines.

At times, I sit back and wonder just how powerful of a movement Marcus Garvey could have had if he could post on YouTube weekly. How much more of a push could Martin Luther King Jr. have had if he had tweets going out daily? Imagine the platform that Bro. Malcolm would have had the gram with powerful images to go with his fiery words. But in hindsight, the beauty of their power and the reach they were able to amass is even more remarkable because it was not about that in the end. Keep your intentions pure, and people will be drawn to how genuine you are in your convictions.

"If you live for the cheers, the boos will kill you."

# LAW 4

Take the Initiative

(Go Getter, Go Getter)

Law 4: Take the Initiative (Go Getter, Go Getter)

I Got it; I Got it

Do not wait to be told every little thing to do, especially in moments when you know better. Step up and take charge of the situation. This is what Leadership is. Being a leader can be as simple as seeing an issue to be addressed. Do not wait for someone else in the world to create a device, app, or tool to fix it. YOU are the one to use your mental power and the resources around you to start the process of thinking of ways to correct the matter. That one gem is worth thousands, if not millions, of dollars because this is what these multibillion-dollar companies have done. The founders saw a need to be tended to, and they took the bull by the horns and did something about it. Leadership does not have to be grand, in any case. You can start as simply as seeing something around your home or school that needs to be straightened, and if it is within your power to do it, why not? You have to cultivate that trait now in the little things. If you are one of the youths reading this, you know when the dishes are stacking up and the trash can need to be emptied. Do not just pass it forty times in one day, waiting for someone else to do it, or in the worst case, your parents fuss at you to do it. I used to tell my young clients that if they feel their parents fuss at them all the time, try to beat them to the punch. Look around your room or home and try to put yourself into the mind of your parents. What do they usually get on your time about? What are some of the main things your teachers gain from you weekly? If you are the job, you know what your higher-ups are like and what they expect from you; how could you jump the gun on them? As a parent, I can tell you there is nothing like walking into the house after a long day of work and everything is complete. What a concept, right? This simple concept holds true in all forms of Leadership. You are almost trying to be a mind reader on what your team needs and what you could do about it before anyone else even thinks of it. That makes you stand out amongst others.

Lead from The Front

Most great leaders in battle, ball, and business are front runners; they lead from the front of the pack. Leadership is not about sitting back and finger-pointing. The best is hands-on and boots on the ground as much as possible. There is just something about seeing a leader willing to get down and dirty in the mix with you that makes you want to increase your production. Good leaders will never ask someone else to do something they have not or would not do themselves. When I see the best players on sports teams, they are known for being the first ones at the practice arena and the last to leave. Think about how a bench player could come to practice late and not put in extra work when the team's heart and soul put it all on the line. It becomes contagious.

Oops! Did I do that?

One trait you must pick up on early on your journey is the willingness to be wrong. Even if it is just taking the "perception" of being wrong in moments, you know in your heart that you are right. You have to be able to grin and bear it, as they say. When you are the leader and the face of something, you have to think that things go fantastically because of the staff and the team. When things go array, it is because of yourself. We see this a lot with superstars in post-game interviews. They are quick to take a load of blame even if the last play had nothing to do with them because this is one of the great attributes of Leadership. Another side to this conversation is if you are the first to do something that has not been done, sure, things are bound to happen that you did not plan to. Yes, it will be placed squarely on your shoulders as it should be. I would advise getting used to saying it is okay if something is not perfect. You have to be able to put your pride and ego to the side to accomplish this. As my mentor says, "simple, but not easy." Like all things in life, you must start very small and work your way to more detrimental moments to build yourself up.

# LAW 5

Be A Trendsetter

(Make Your Wave)

Law 5: Be A Trendsetter (Make Your Wave)

Be a thermostat, NOT the thermometer

Let us do a quick pop quiz…Ready…Great. Question 1: What is a thermostat? Take your time, no rush. Got it? Ok cool. Now, question 2: What is a thermometer? Come on…you got this...Got it written? Bet! Now, we can continue. You see, we are ALL made of energy. We and all of our powers interact, whether you notice it or not. It is always happening a million times per day. So, when you walk into a room, you do one of two things. My point in this book section is to heighten your awareness so you can take control of it right now as you read this. Upon entering a space, your two choices are to be reactive to the energy already present before your arrival. Like a sponge, you feed off the attitudes, vibes, and body language of the people in the room. The other option is to SET the room's tone with your energy and make them react to you. I love to use sports as examples because they are easy to relate to most demographics. In most sports, it is always to your advantage to make your opponent react to you versus you reacting and responding to what they want you to do.

It is the same thing in everyday life. As a leader, you have to cultivate the mindset that it doesn't matter what took place in your personal life before arriving, it doesn't matter if your car broke down on the way, it doesn't matter if your boyfriend/girlfriend blocked you on Instagram this morning. When I cross the threshold of this building, I will bring so much energy and warmth with my sheer presence. Trust me, try it one day. Go to your class or your job with an extra pep to your step. Walk with your shoulders back and chin up. Make eye contact with people as you pass them and honestly greet them as it matters. Just watch how people start to notice and respond to you.

Observe the people who start to draw to you naturally. I am not speaking about some hocus pocus magic trick; this is how things in life work. You want to be the thermostat in the room. Set the temperature of your workspace, classroom, and home. Do not use the thermometer, which only reacts to the temperature on the side. Do not be the energy sponge that lets the grumpy lady serving grits throw your entire morning. Leaders set the tone.

In sports, you will hear announcers say all the time that the team takes on the identity of their coach. Mike Tyson even went further in hindsight, thinking about the years he lived with his coach. He said he was a teenager but dressed and acted like an older white man. Even down to his haircut and how he would speak. In that example, he was the sponge, but it shows you the power his coach had unbeknownst to him. I want you to know it and own it.

First, they love you, and then they hate you. Then they love you again.

When I think of some of the most outstanding leaders of all time, at one point or another, they were most likely clowned, laughed at, and hated by others. You have to know that when you are trying to be a trendsetter and go against the grain of whatever one else around you are doing, you are like an alien to them. It is human nature to set patterns you can identify in all parts of your life. You want to be able to put people into cute little boxes so you do not have to spend mental energy relearning people time and time again. The downfall to that attribute is that when we see something that does not fit into the box, we feel we should have an adverse reaction to it. As a leader, you are breaking the old mold. You are going into uncharted territory like the man trying to navigate the great ocean at the time when they thought the world was flat! You are going to fall off the side. They would jab at you until someone was bold enough and had the heart to do it. This is how we must be as leaders. You set yourself apart. You think differently, speak differently, dress in your own fashion, and do not carry yourself like anyone else around. This is what most of the great leaders did. As you prove yourself and have consistency in your dealings, the laughter fades, and people become curious about how you managed to pull it off. They want to copy you; they want to imitate. This may feel bad at first, and no one likes to be mocked, but when it comes to Leadership, this may be the very thing you want. In basketball, they say that the point guard is the extension of the coach on the floor. Or look at football. It is the quarterback that has to embody the coach's concepts and character. This is how we want our fellow teammates and coworkers in the realm of Leadership.

"It's easy to be a zombie or a robot, and it's a hard road being a free thinker." – Sean P.

# AFTERWORD

# Afterword

## By Raymond Dockery III

An age-old adage begs the question, "Are leaders born or are leaders made?" The inquiry is highly debated among scholars, psychologists, sociologists, and many professions stretching across spectrums. Likewise, the same probe sparks contemplation and conversation in barbershops, beauty salons, educational institutions, homes, and inevitably, in the very synapses of thoughts. No matter which side of the perspective one stands on, it produces both points and counterpoints, lists of reasons, and staunch firmness of viewpoints. The more profound question involves why that initial question matters so much in the first place. Though arriving at the solution may not be so simple, the answer is clear: whether born a leader or made into one, anyone who desires to be a leader wants to be extraordinary in Leadership. This is where the 'Laws of Leadership' sets itself apart as essential and beneficial.

You see, Leadership is not a one-dimensional arena. In all actuality, the state or position of being a leader is immersed in the actions that incite guidance, authority, and direction in whatever facet that pertains to you. That detrimental key is that it is an inside job, and 'Born' or 'made' is of no consequence. Experience over time, proper perception, repetitive, perfected practice, and appropriate training are skills that can be obtained, developed, and honed. The crux of the matter is that those mentioned above must originate with you. A wise man once told me, "Change your mind, and you will change your life!" It doesn't matter if it's the military, school, the local church, the neighborhood, or home; you have to embrace that you are already a leader or becoming one!

 Situations, circumstances, and life will all cause different and often varied types of Leadership. While many of these will affect us, the style of leader you are heavily depends on 'Who' you intend on serving in conjunction with your How and Why. Too often, when Leadership is ill-equipped, it is conveyed as a measure to make others aid you. Great leaders learn that their focus and intent must be to serve others. This is important because Leadership is not a popularity contest. Sometimes, being a leader means making an unpopular choice that will not provide fodder for clout chasers. Simply stated: try not to fixate your mindset on Leadership being some numeric equation that is narrowly compacted into a science. Instead, utilize the tools provided as a paintbrush, and your Leadership will become an art.

In conclusion, I sincerely hope that if you are reading this right now, your very next steps are to take the information and decide to take the initiative. If you fancy yourself a "Go-Getter," just know that the first part of that esteemed moniker is 'GO.' Not even faith can be operated without taking action. So, I think you are ready now. You know. You have the steps. You have the tools, and–YOU HAVE WHAT IT TAKES! A sphere of influence and a world in dire straits is looking for its' next wave. Be the trendsetter of the changes you desire to see. Impact the minds that will spark creativity. Whether you become the next 'Drum major for justice' or become the newest constituent of being resolved to achieve 'by any means necessary,' start, serve, initiate trend set…LEAD.

Points to Consider:

At this point of the book, I always love to ask questions and get the reader's mind moving because, honestly, reading can be a passive activity, depending on how you do it. So, I love to ask questions at the end of my book to make some of the high points stick long after you put them down.

1. Before leading others, how well do you say you regularly have discipline and control over yourself? If you lack faith in this area, write down what hinders you and how you could work on it.

2. If you read this leadership publication, you may already be in a leadership role. What was your intent when you decided to lead others? Where do you want to lead them to?

3. In this question to yourself, be honest. Do you ever find yourself doing things specifically for social media to get credit for it? If so, what feelings do you think you are after in these moments? How could you go about it differently in future situations?

4. Do you find yourself to be a person who naturally steps up and takes the initiative on things you see to be done, or do you most likely wait until you are instructed on what to do?

5. Do you try to be a trendsetter, or do you tend to try to blend in as best you can with the group? Do you usually operate like a thermometer or a thermostat?

# Expanding Your Vision:
## The Heroes Journey
By: Seanathan Polidore, MSP

**Table of Contents:**

Acknowledgments………………………184

Dedication……………………………....186

Foreword: Dorrian Wilson……………...187

Foreword Remix: Kofi Piese…………...190

Introduction: Dillan Monette……………………………196

Episode 1: Origin Story………………...200

Episode 2: Seeing New Worlds (The Need for Travel)……………………………....205

Episode 3: Finding Your Sensei (Mentorship)……………………………209

Episode 4: Changing Your Environment…………………………....215

Episode 5: Fighting YourVillain………..219

Episode 6: Bringing It Back Home……..227

Afterword: Raymond Dockery III……....232

Acknowledgments:

I want to thank God, the grand creator, for my health, mind, and the determination that was placed in my heart to complete these projects. I have to always acknowledge the power greater than myself first. Next, I would like to acknowledge my beautiful wife. At the time of writing this, she is stepping out on faith as a brand-new business owner. Coming from where we are from, this takes a ton of vision. It very much expanded from the norm. You are currently walking what I am about to type right now. I want to always acknowledge my family and friends because you push, motivate, and spur me on to keep doing my process to have these books rolling out. Sometimes in life, you can feel as if you are talking or writing to yourself, but having a strong support team to show you glimpses of hope Makes it all worth it. I want to take the time to thank my young readers. If you are a young reader picking this book up, maybe this is your first time cracking open a book outside of your schoolwork. Perhaps this book will be the first to give you an intellectual sense of accomplishment. I can still remember being 19 in the U.S. Navy when an older gentleman introduced me to the enchanting world of books. I clearly remember the feeling I felt when I turned to the last page of my first novel. I could hardly believe it, and I wanted to tell everyone about it. I had been an athlete my whole life and only knew of the joy of making a jump shot. Never would I have dreamed I could feel that way about books. That was the most life-changing moment for me. At 38 now, I still chase that feeling of the first time. I pray this book serves you the same. Keep your eyes, heart, and mind open. As my big brother says, Mind UP.

Dedication:

As I am writing this, I realize that it is about a week away from the day that my grandmother made her transition into the afterlife two years ago. I have to dedicate this book to her because she was the most optimistic and open-minded person I have ever met in my life. She embodied having an expanded vision. She may not have traveled all over the world, but she always had this huge global view and a tremendous hope that everything would work itself out in the end, no matter what. As time goes by, I miss that more and more as this world gets crazier and out of hand week by week. Being a forty-year educator, you were always very serious about proper writing and speaking ability. You made it your life work to help your students, and anyone around you realizes that communication skills could get you very far in life. If you have pride in yourself and your word choices, then others will respect you as well. I am telling you now; I get it, maw maw. I love you and miss you dearly. I live to make you and Pawpaw proud of me.

# OG
# FOREWORD

Foreword: Dorrian Wilson

Dear Readers,

Hello. I hope this forward finds you safe, healthy, and COMPLETELY UNCOMFORTABLE. That's right, I said it! I am sure that has taken you off guard but bear with me for a bit. You'll see that I'm not entirely crazy and that buying this book is the most precious gift you could have given yourself. You'll see.

I have known Seanathan Polidore since high school. At this point, it means 20+ years, give or take a memory or two. He is a very dear friend. A staple in my life at every turn, be it a good decision, bad decision, indecision, or just plain restlessness. We all know that space where nothing fits anymore. The blinders are off. Our once pristine view of life has dissipated like a fog to reveal that everything around you isn't so perfect. There are chips and cracks, and like any shoe that no longer fits.... your heel hangs over the bottom. In that restlessness, you begin to question everything you know. I know I did. Was I the bird, or was I the cage? It is hard to know the difference when who you are, your identity at the moment, is enmeshed with the things around you. Your town, family, work, and relationships. It is all one thing. My dreams did not know what it was like to stand alone. To exist without the thought of someone else in mind until I decided to fly. Take the hero's journey. Only when you can finally see things and the things around you for what they are can you see so many other things, too. A way out. In this book, Seanathan is finally sharing all the wonderful words he has shared with me over the years. They have proven to be the fuel that keeps me going, the parachute that softens my landings, and the cape the world sees coming to save the day. So, go ahead and expand your vision. Hell, even take the hero's journey. All the tools you need are in the pages ahead. Fly! I dare you.

# FOREWORD REMIX

# Foreword Remix: Kofi Piesie

Before I begin this foreword, I want to define the word "vision" and look at its etymology. According to the online Oxford Dictionary, 1. vision is the faculty or state of being able to see. 2. the ability to think about or plan the future with imagination or wisdom.

Okay, now let's look at the etymology for the word "vision" in the online etymology dictionary, but first, you may ask what etymology is. In short form, it is nothing more than the root of a word, the origin, and sometimes the meaning changes throughout history. Vision, according to the etymology dictionary, is c. 1300, "something seen in the imagination or in the supernatural," from Anglo-French visioun, Old French vision "presence, sight; view, look, appearance; dream, supernatural sight" (12c.), from Latin visionem (nominative visio) "act of seeing, sight, thing seen," noun of action from past participle stem of videre "to see," from PIE root *weid- "to see." The meaning "sense of sight" was first recorded in the late 15c. Meaning "statesman-like foresight, political sagacity" is attested from 1926. This word, vision, has not changed throughout history as many words do. We see words like sight, view, see, dream, and especially imagination. Your imagination, which is your faculty or action, forms ideas or gives you the ability to create pictures in your mind. These pictures or visions only you can see in your mind. Everyone you share your ideas with will not see it and will most likely try to talk you out of whatever work entails to manifest your vision. Your vision is your vision and no one else, so don't let it matter if they don't believe it or not. Don't let them stop your process or change your mind from putting in the work or not believing in your vision.

Manifest Your Vision into Reality

I want to share some of the steps it will take to manifest your vision and expand it. First, you must write down a step-by-step plan for reaching that vision and pulling those ideas from the spiritual to the physical. Second, you will have to research things online that align with your vision; you will have to look at tons of videos that align with your vision and take classes, even if that's enrolling in a college or trade school. Third, pay for information from someone with years of experience and find a mentor who can guide you and give you good instructions on what not to do and what to do. A mentor can share his mistakes, and you can bypass those mistakes on your journey to get your vision out, which can manifest much faster and be a success much quicker.

Sacrifices Must Be Made

Sacrifices must be made to see your vision in real time, literally. I am going to drop a shortlist of things we must sacrifice.

List

1. Time

2. Hanging out every weekend

3 Your Pleasures

A lot of us have jobs and put in a lot of time on the job, which is someone else's vision they took and materialized. Remember, the etymology of vision also means "dream." We will give all our time to make sure someone else's dreams stay alive and want give birth to our own dreams. If you work on a job 8, 10, or 12 hours a week, I suggest once you get home, sacrifice some of your sleep time and invest in getting out your vision. On your days off, sacrifice unproductive time like hanging out with the fellas or the ladies to shoot the breeze like the old folks used to say. Use that time to work, work, and work on your dreams. Sacrificing your pleasure like smoking, drinking, and television is a must. Those are also unproductive things to be doing, and becoming inebriated can slow or stop you in your tracks from making you a little closer to getting out your vision. I see so many people committing hours and hours of watching television daily. Make a sacrifice by cutting some of those television hours in half.

Traveling Is One Of The Greatest Forms of Education

Traveling is something you need to add to your step-by-step plan. Traveling to conferences, lectures, and master classes will help you tremendously, trust me. Traveling, meeting new people, and building relationships with those you meet can help you. Like-minded people can motivate and inspire you. The Experience of traveling and attending things, in my opinion, is the best form of education. The plus of traveling is that it could open your eyes to more and help you expand that vision bigger and better than you could imagine.

Remember, your vision is for you, and let nothing or no one stop your vision. Take the necessary steps to achieve those ideas from your vision.

# INTRODUCTION

Introduction: Ashely Wade

Good People,

The beauty in this book relies entirely on the connection between personal challenges and triumphs faced in life. We don't really take the time to see how events relate to each other, how thought processes relate to each other, and how life events relate to each other. We are often on the back side, constantly catching up to things that happen TO us. In this reflection, we realize that our life needs vision. One must know that it's possible to create the vision of the life you want to experience. One also has to BELIEVE that you Can have the Life you want to Experience. If you have awareness and Pay Attention, the Steps AND the Manifestations will Appear in Your Human Experience. Have you taken time to visualize the person that you want to be? Don't run past that last sentence. Re-read it. Have you taken time to figure out who you are as a person and your Personal Value? That's why I love the significance of the book title. "Expanding Your Vision" will challenge you to expand the vision you have of yourself and your life in different ways. Why is this necessary, you may ask. My response is that we are multi-dimensional human beings. There should be depth, perspective, and awareness in how you see yourself AND the world. 2019-2021 I was deeply challenged by my spiritual leader, and one of the biggest realizations I had during that time was realizing that I did not believe in myself as much as I thought I did. I believed in myself for the "regular." I wrestled with this concept because, by this time, I had accomplished what I thought was my wildest dream, and that was becoming a pharmacist. I'm not minimizing this feat because it took a great deal of belief and resilience to achieve educationally, especially my Doctorate Degree in Pharmacy. And as I'm writing, it just hit me. I now understand why they say God's Will is not our Will because WE think so low and basic of ourselves as People AND our Abilities. But Low Vibration is not our Birthright. Use what you know about Yourself thus far as a baseline, and use these upcoming gems as building blocks for the Person you want to BE and the future you want to SEE.

Lastly, Be Confident as you walk through the Portals as they Appear as if you were on a journey. Life can demonstrate Infinite Possibilities if you See it that way.

Continue to Seek and Be Light, So You Can Be You and Max That Shit Out. -

Dr. Ashley Wade
Pharmacist, Author, Curator, Griotte.

# EPISODE 1

Episode 1: Origin Story

Humble Beginnings

Research some of your favorite superheroes and celebrities, and you will see that the common trend amongst them all started from the humblest beginnings. If you are in a spot in your life where you feel you wish your family had more money, were born with more talent, or had gone to a better school, I have some great news for you! You see, according to every superhero story, you are in the perfect spot. Some of the most famous superstars you may know of today at some points have been homeless. They have been bankrupt and emotionally broken. They had the experience of loneliness, cold, hunger, and eating out of a trash can in some instances. It is only a part of the process. All of these setbacks set you up for the comebacks. What do you think gave them the audacity to imagine themselves in a grand place despite their harsh reality? Tyler Perry, Eric Thomas, Idris Alba, and the list continues. All of these stars have seen their share of time hungry and homeless. Do you know what made them keep pushing in their darkest moments? VISION! The pictures that they were able to create in their mind about their future surpassed the things that were happening in their physical reality at the time. Let us start with yourself. Ask yourself, what gets you going in the morning? What keeps you up at night with anticipation? What do you believe you do better than most? These are some of the fundamental questions that you must ask yourself to begin your journey to greatness. You must keep these pillars in front of your mind at all times. Your circumstance does not have to be your final destination. You CAN create the life that you want. The picture you see in your mind's eye can be yours if you are brave and bold enough to take it.

Next, let us take a moment to define what we mean when we use a phrase like "Expanding Your Vision." Start with the term expand. The Webster dictionary will tell you that the word expands means to increase in size, extent, and volume. To spread or stretch out. When you define the word vision, you are not speaking about your literal ability to see with your eyes. We are talking about the second definition that you will find under this word which is the act or power of anticipating that which will or may come to pass. When I speak of expanding your vision, I want you to increase, stretch, and expand your imaginative anticipation of what is to come for yourself and your family. Dream Big and Dream Bold! Do not play yourself small because shrinking yourself does not help the world! Imagine if you could do anything you want, and time and money were not an issue. What does that look like in your mind? How does it feel when you picture it? That is your vision. Write it. Draw it. Make the picture of it as clear as you can to yourself. You are the hero of your journey, but every hero must have direction and instruction to get to them on the right path. This brings me to my next topic. Finding mentorship.

I can remember my teenage years clearly. Wishing all the time that I was taller because my peers were sprouting up around me. Wishing I went to a better school that had more exposure because at the time I was a basketball player who had the hoop dreams of playing ball for a really big national rank college someday. I could feel the emotions I felt looking around at other guys from other situations and thinking, Man if only I had what they had. These are very natural thoughts so do not feel bad if they cross your mind from time to time. My point in this section of the book is simply to make you aware of them and to help you move forward in a more positive direction from that thought. Instead of feeling like you are the weak victim in the story, I want you to see that you are actually in a position of power.

# EPISODE 2

## Episode 2: Finding Your Sensei (Mentorship)

Once you have identified your vision and gained the courage to take on the unique mission that the creator has carved out for you must find the correct guide to help you hone your skills. Another part of every hero's journey is that moment when they find their grandmaster. They have that instructor who enlightens the pupil on all of the wonderful hidden talents and abilities that are embedded within them.  In The Karate Kid, Danielson had Mr. Miyagi. In the Star Wars adventure, Luke Skywalker had Obi-Wan Kenobi, and in the smash hit The Matrix, Neo had the illustrious Morpheus. These Master teachers are not meant to walk the journey for you. They are simply there to light the path only you can walk for yourself.  In your search for a mentor, you want to seek someone already on the journey you would like to take on. If possible, you want to find someone who has experienced success and failures. These mentors can streamline your process because they can tell you everything, they wish they had done differently when they were in the same spot where you are today.

This crash course of experience alone can save you double-digit years of "figuring it out" and thousands of dollars in mistakes if you take heed to the advice given. If you feel as if you do not know any suitable mentors around you, do not have limited vision. Use the power of technology at your disposal. You can find thousands of people from all walks of life who may be more than willing to exchange information and ideas with you from abroad IF you have the courage and persistence to ask.

Remember, in every hero story, the wise guide gives the hero all the tools they need to finally take on the big bad villain in the climax. You must invest your time and resources into finding the one most suited for your needs. Most of the best coaching and instruction will have a cost attached to them. It may be monetary, and at other times, it will be a cost of a different nature, but whatever it is, you must be willing to sacrifice as much as possible because the lessons can be simply priceless on your journey of development.

People who follow my content often notice how much I harp on mentorship. Well, that is because I think that is the most critical element of my life that has given me the most return. The ability to find amazing coaching in all aspects of my life, the ability to use what they give me, and then the most important aspect is mentoring others. "To teach is to learn twice" is another one of my all-time favorite quotes. As you pass on knowledge to someone else you are reinforcing things to yourself while reevaluating your perspective on some area that may assist you in understanding the subject on a deeper level.

# EPISODE 3

## Episode 3: Seeing New Worlds (The Need for Travel)

The next part in the process of expanding your vision is to travel away from the environment to which you have become accustomed. At some point in every hero story, the main character has to leave their family and friends whom they have known their whole life to adventure off into a dream world of some sort. Whether it is an odyssey into outer space, a trip to never never land, or another dimension in time. The creators of these great tales knew it was important for their audience to see the hero leaving their physical comfort zone to be challenged by new terrain, creatures, and wonders. This journey that we are speaking of becomes the middle section of most major blockbuster films. In this section of the story, the protagonist will be challenged the most. It is in this strange land that the hero will finally connect and fully commit to what it is that he was created to do. Traveling is one of the greatest forms of education. No amount of schooling can match what you learn consciously and subconsciously from traveling. You will meet people who will help you blossom and change your worldview. You will see awe-inspiring sights that will help you put your life in a better perspective. Remember, once your mind is expanded, it can never return to its original dimensions. After you have traveled and experienced some of the things that life has to offer, you can return to your community and effectively pour back into the ones who never took the opportunity to venture out the way you have.

I know what your next thought is. Well, Sean, I flat out cannot afford to travel at the moment. I get it, trust me. Keep in mind earlier in the text, I mentioned the importance of investing in yourself at times. When it comes to travel, this topic indeed falls within that category. Try to start small if possible. It does not have to be that far away. Try to save up some money and take the bus a few cities away. Move up and try to take a train further out. Ultimately graduate by flying out of state. The more you do this process, the more you will gain confidence in your ability to save up and achieve a goal, and also, you will become bolder going into distant places alone at times. It's hard to explain in words how much your entire DNA shifts when you are enjoying foods you have never heard of before, waking up to new sights, and feeling an atmosphere that is completely foreign to where you are from. When you return home, you may be like a fish out of water for a few days. It will take some adjusting because once you have lived through a different experience, you will yearn to have that feeling more and more often. This is a life-changing moment in your journey because you will be at a crossroads. Either it is time to pack up and leave altogether which we will cover in our next chapter, or you will have to try to create those moments you enjoyed so much where you are now. You have to shift your thinking to pull off this feat. I mean, maybe you cannot afford to buy the latest Jordans when they release. Maybe you have to hold off on the newest iPhone, but the rewards of brand-new experiences will serve you far more than material things in the grand scheme of things. Your mental shift will come in the way of what you are willing to sacrifice to achieve your goals in life. Let us continue expanding our vision on the subject of travel. Even if you cannot afford to travel on a small scale, you can read, watch films, and study documentaries about faraway lands.

With your handy dandy smartphone, you can travel as far as you would like to go absolutely free and still broaden your scope of life by educating yourself about how this world functions outside of your day-to-day environment. Do not settle for the things going on at the school you attend. Do not just lock in on what happens on your block or the city you reside in. There is a vast world out there waiting for the taking. My mentor always told me about what he called "triple darkness." You do not know; you don't know that you don't know. Being lost and oblivious to what is around you. You do not want to exist in that space. Keep expanding to the light.

So, how did I go about experiencing my travels, you may be thinking? The answer is relatively simple. The U.S. Navy. That is right; many people do not realize that I am a U.S. Navy veteran. Once I graduated high school and that basketball scholarship to that big-ranking school never manifested, I had to transition into another field. This could be a chapter of an entirely different book within itself, "Calling an Audible." Nevertheless, I joined the military a week after I graduated, and this afforded me the ability to visit 23 countries, meet people from all over the world on the ships I was stationed on, and forced me to accelerate my learning process of making it in this big world on my own with no family for thousands of miles to save me. I had the opportunity to be stationed on both coasts of the country, and I attended boot camp and Naval school in the Midwest. So, this was a wealth of hands-on experiences in four years. This may sound like a long time, but when you think about it, four years is a flash in the pan compared to the entirety of your whole life. When I returned home after my tour, I was a very different person than the young, wide-eyed, lost kid who had left. I gained global knowledge, and I had a very detailed understanding of how life works versus the assumptions I made based on my limited surroundings. Once again, I am not saying I have the perfect answer to every life issue you may have. In this series of books, I only want to offer the experiences that helped me become a better version of myself, and I pray that at least one tip will be a life-altering moment for you.

# EPISODE 4

Episode 4: Change Your Environment

In this section of the hero's journey, we discuss changing your environment for further progress. From birth until you graduate high school, your parents have taken care of your night and day in the best manner that they could. Home is where the heart comes to mind. All the familiar faces are in your city. You want to go where everyone knows your name and all that jazz. But sometimes, along your journey of developing yourself and evolving, you may have to face the idea that you must uproot yourself to be nurtured in the fashion required for your ultimate success. During a critical phase in your development, you notice that the people you grew up with may not be on the same page as you for whatever reason. There is nothing wrong with that and not saying anything bad about them, but they are no longer emotionally or mentally feeding you, which IS bad. When you relocate to a different place, you might find that the pocket of people you need to groom you for the next level of life is across the state. Maybe It is a completely different region of the country, but you will never know if you are not willing to be comfortable and leave your happy surroundings. This is where the above chapter about traveling comes in handy. As you travel and venture out further from your home, you begin to notice the wonders away from your city, but you also start to realize the distinct differences in mindsets and personalities in different regions. The more you experience these moments, the more you slowly realize that the key opportunity you may need to reach your goals may be planted in better soil elsewhere.

When I speak of changing your environment, let us not be shortsighted and only think about physical locations. I am also talking about people, places, and things in your life. Becoming the hero you want to be very well may require you to completely change your choice in the activities that you currently love to indulge in. You may have to find better selections of music and movies. Changing your environment might look like rearranging your circle of friends that you may have had most of your life. Becoming a better version of yourself will require you to leave your old self. I know all of those old people and old activities served you up to this point in your life, but your ability to put those things down will be a huge indicator of the level of success that you can reach. As you ascend to a higher level, you will have to realize that you will have to cut out the people and things that are not serving you toward your large picture for yourself. Another part of expanding your vision will be protecting your vision at all costs. If you don't, you will find yourself heavily distracted with anger, low energy, and anxiety because you will feel that you are in an inner battle with yourself.

"A journey of a thousand steps begins with one step."

-Ancient Chinese Proverb

# EPISODE 5

Episode 5: Fighting Your Villain (Darth Vader)

This may be the most difficult part of the text to digest. I always hate to be the bearer of bad news, but as a writer and a speaker, I pride myself on being as real as possible. I never want to paint false expectations for anyone. I would much rather you be equipped with the tools to handle yourself rather than avoid these types of moments altogether. After you figure out what your gift is in this world. You have found a master to teach you. You take on the journey and travel a bit. You gain the courage to leave home and step out on faith. Everything is going to be perfect, right? You've followed all of the above steps. NOPE!!! There will be the big bad villain you have to face. We have all seen this tale time and time again. At some point, the hero has to face the ultimate bad guy. In Star Wars, you have Darth Vader. In the Matrix series, Neo is fighting Mr. Smith. Those are just comics and movies. In real life, if you are a teen reading this, your grand enemy may look like fighting to graduate. Maybe you come from a rough upbringing and surroundings, and you are just trying to escape that world and live a more "normal" life. Some people have what feel like enemies INSIDE of them if you have physical, emotional, and behavioral issues that you literally can't control, such as ADD, bipolar, or depression. It may show its evil head-like physical handicaps to your body, and you just CAN'T function quite like everyone else. No matter your story, the battle is ALL YOURS, and the whole world is waiting for you to step up and face the villain mano e mano. Your mentors, teachers, and parents can only provide you with the tools you will need in life, but they can't walk the path for you. They have had their share of villains they had to endure. This battle for your life is on YOU. Put into your mind firmly now that no one is coming to save you! There is no one coming to swoop down and save the day in this film…the savior you are looking for is inside of YOU!

For my adult readers, I'm sure your monsters can look different altogether. Your enemies look like they can look like the bills on your counter. It may be past or current relationship situations. The villain that haunts your sleep can be your job. Forty hours a week, it's waiting for you to clock into a weight on your shoulders. You know your war. You know that thing that makes you toss and turn at night when the lights go out? What disturbs your peace when you should be in your most relaxed moments ever? The thoughts that creep into your mind when you are trying to be present with your kids or your spouse. THAT'S HIM! How are you going to face it? This one obstacle can be a detour for the rest of your life and your family's life. Now is the time to bite down and plant your feet. Decide to run no more and be the hero that you were designed to become.

It does not matter if you are a teen or an adult; the final fight is always a bloody and nasty war. This will not be pretty by any stretch of the imagination. It may feel at times that you may lose your life under the crushing blows of the opposition.

Two summers ago, my villain popped up on the scene. Out of the blue as most good villains do. I guess you can say in a sense I am still fighting my archrival to this day. For some people, their monster will be killed in one big swing, and for others, it will be an ongoing process to overcome and survive. The big, bad, creepy boss I had to fight in my journey was the death of my grandmother. I guess it's safe to say since I was a little boy, the death of my grandparents was something that always loomed in the back of my mind. Since birth, my grandparents have played such a large role in my life. I spent so much of my childhood in their bed. For some reason, I had a great understanding of the concept of death at an early age. I would toss and turn, thinking about losing them. How would I feel? How would I make it in this world without them? What would the funeral be like? I even actually had nightmares about my grandfather's funeral in particular. It's one of those dreams where it starts in the middle, and you don't know what's going on just yet. I'm in this church, and people are seated already; I don't know why I'm not. People have their heads down, and I see the casket in the front of the church. I don't know WHO it is, though. I walk up by myself. Slowly. The walk feels a mile long. Then I looked inside, and it was him. God, I popped out of that dream so fast. Two years ago, things were not dreams anymore. The phone calls to come home and see her were real. The calls about how things were NOT going well were real. Seeing her in the bed at her absolute worst was too real for my mind and heart to shake. I think beyond those pains; seeing my grandfather so broken up emotionally rocked me more than I could ever explain on this keyboard right now. Up until this point in my life, I was blessed not to have experienced a serious loss like this before. The morning that dreadful call came; all I could feel was numb. Lost. confused. Everything was a blur. Hazy. I couldn't focus on anything. All the phone calls and messages came rushing in, but I couldn't get my mind around taking any of them in. I was full out in the first stage of Grief. The first of the five stages is denial. You know it's happening, and its reality, but your brain can't process it. Walking down to that funeral home with my family was real. The tears are real. The sights and sounds I can hear it. Then I'm at the casket, by myself. I look inside. She's there. Forever there. I can't do that thing that we all do to pop ourselves out of our sleep back into reality. This was my new reality. My 800lbs monster was not firmly on my back. That monster was grief. Every person handles grief in their own way. Like most movies, when the hero initially takes on the villain, the bad guys start off KICKING HIS BUTT! I was getting crushed, and it seemed like a one-sided fight for a while to all who observed me. I was hulked smashed, Thanos snapped and Kilmonger kicked. There is no set-in-stone way to deal with the loss of a loved one, and in this publication, I am not claiming to provide one. As always, all I can do is tell you what has worked for me, and you can see if it applies to your situation. The second stage of grief is anger. I was furious. Angry at any and everything for no good reason on any given day. If you know me, that is not my natural personality whatsoever, but this was an outlier situation. It felt like there was no person that I could talk to take the pain from me. Most places I tried to go to for an escape didn't help. I felt myself sinking into the third stage, which is depression. Oddly enough, I figured out a way for me to fight back. This was my chance to strike a major blow against this terror. I revisited my childhood love. Martial arts. I found that going to martial arts class became like moving meditation for me because when trying to avoid being punched in the face, it's pretty hard for your mind to drift off somewhere else. It forced me to be present at the moment. It allowed me to let out my anger and frustration in a safe environment and have the comrade of the team that you are training, sweating, and bleeding with. I found my way to beat down the monster. Of course, I still have my horrible days and nights where I feel depression trying to slip back on my back, and I have moments when my grandmother crosses my mind, and I want to cry, but I was able to function and press on with life. For some of us, that IS victory. This is the championship, and this is the giant sword in the villain's chest that makes him disappear at the climax. Survival. Each of us must define survival for ourselves no matter what battle we face. You have to find your weapon of choice to win, and nobody can decide that for you.

# EPISODE 6

Episode 6: Bringing It Back Home

Now, this is a great part of any story. When the hero slays the big dangerous dragon, he returns to the village. After you have traveled and gained countless experiences and you have overcome your obstacles you must come back and share with your community the lessons you've gained along the way. Now you are in the position to BE the mentor to someone else. You can go out and pour your gems and nuggets into the up-and-coming pupils that you see getting ready to start their respective journeys, and you see that memory in your mind when you were in the same position. You remember thinking you knew everything and looking back on how much you didn't know. You recall not being able to imagine just how big and wide this world is based on the area that was your day-to-day stomping grounds. This recollection helps you to connect to others better since you have been in shoes just like theirs. When it comes to bringing it back to the community where you are from, out of all the places I've been blessed to speak and do events, nothing feels like having the chance to do it in the city where I'm from. This city was raised for good and bad. The man I am today was shaped and molded by these schools, churches, libraries, coaches, gyms, etc. I feel I must share anything I've picked up along the way back into the very place that supplied my foundation as a man. I encourage you as you take on your journey and seek out mentorship to keep your future pupils in mind. This will help you to learn and retain information better if you learn a skill with the possibility of having to teach it to someone else in mind. Keep in mind that every challenge you face in life isn't necessarily about you every time. It is self-centered to think so. Sometimes, the adversity you encounter is to give you the tools you will need to help someone else in the future. As the years roll by, I have become the OG in a lot of rooms that I am in. I feel obligated to pour knowledge and wisdom into anyone in the room willing to lend an ear.

As I mentioned, I was blessed to travel to 23 countries in the U.S. Navy. After my naval duty, I moved to Atlanta, GA, for a few years. When I returned home in 04' it was an amazing thing. The same city I was born and raised in was different to my mind's eye now. The people, buildings, and food were the same, but I was a different person. Now, I had gone from boy to man. I hit the ground running and tried my hand at giving back in every way that was within my capacity. While living in Atlanta, I had become a fitness coach, so that would be my entry point to giving back. I did fitness and health demonstrations for schools, I helped train football teams, and I trained countless people in the surrounding area. Next, that evolved into speaking at schools about the importance of reading and test-taking skills to improve their L.E.A.P scores. I was even invited a few times to help motivate the school staff to tackle their up-and-coming school year. Now, my giving back is in the form of the very books you are reading, being able to teach classes, and taking part in panels and groups that help elevate the community at large. You have to find your way to bring something back in the form you feel best. Yes, as I have just demonstrated, that can change forms many times in one lifetime if you are open to growing and evolving. The pride and joy that you feel is a positive pillar in the community and a feeling that is close to indescribable. Just think that as the years go back, most of the leaders you had in your life are starting to transition to the afterlife one by one. All of your favorite teachers, coaches, and city leaders. Now, YOU are that leader. You are someone else's favorite something if you allow yourself to be. You know how it felt to have that one coach or teacher that changed the course of your life. Well, this is your chance to be that for the next generation. You are the hero. You have gained the proper skills, and you have conquered your villain. Now, pass the crown.

# AFTERWORD

## Afterword: Raymond Dockery III

Where there is no vision, the people are unrestrained…

Prov. 29:18 (NASB)

A short, mild-mannered, green-eyed little boy sat intently, captivated by the action happening on the screen of a small gray television. Entranced, he watched as this superhuman with endowed abilities attempted to navigate regular life. It was perplexing the first time I had seen Superman. By himself, he was so much more advanced than those around him. He was stronger, bulletproof, and had heat vision and x-ray vision. Yet, Superman costumed his true self to conceal his identity. Every other hero I had seen was the opposite; they wore costumes to become someone else. To give you a good idea of what I mean: Peter Parker masked up to become Spiderman, but Superman masked up to become Clark Kent.

You might be wondering why this may have seemed to befuddled in the first place. But consider this: while most heroes stumbled upon their abilities or happened upon them situationally or through circumstance, Superman had come to the planet already endowed with power and purpose. I'll be frank while simultaneously quoting Jay-Z: "Man you were who you were 'fore you got here." Like many of you reading, if you have read any of the other prolific books by Seanathan Polidore, you've been equipped. Yet each of us must have his/her vision expanded so that which has been instilled in us manifests to fruition. This type of expansion goes beyond the thought process but graduates you in the process of allowing thought to encompass action en route to achieving goals. Although many people would not consider themselves a hero, I beg to differ. It was once said that if you wanted to hide something from people, all you need to do is put it in a book. Yet here you are: reading, digging, searching, daring to be better, growing, improving, and going beyond your limits! You are proof that every hero has an original story.

You have not only survived, but you have grown. Your humble beginnings have saturated you in experience and forged for you a path steeped in greatness. You're not watching it in a theater or on television; you're living it! Committing to achieving, especially with all the intangibles of this life, my dear reader, is, to me, one of the most heroic things one can do. This process transforms into the one that does what others could but don't, sometimes won't, or can't yet do. Whatever your lane, your destination and path may not be the same. Those who have traveled your path can best guide you. Hence, there is a need for a Mr. Miyagi, Morpheus, Ip Man, or an Obi-Wan; your Sensei has a unique way of illuminating your path and helping you to navigate some of the perils. I know what you're thinking, "but Superman didn't have a Sensei." I get it, except he did. When the man of steel had an issue, he had a mentor who had uploaded a hologram of himself to address any issue Superman may have had. His mentor was his dad Ja-rel. Without mentorship, seeing that new world or changing your environment can become daunting. You'll find that the best mentors/senseis (which is why it's essential to find the best one for you) instill so much value that even when they can't physically reach the gems, they have given life to their mentees.

My favorite scenes in movies and television are when the hero seems down and out, and defeat is both imminent and inevitable. When all hope seems lost, the hero remembers his sensei's teachings and causes the tide to turn for the best. As you have read already, there's an evil Sith Emperor, a Mr. Smith, or a Thanos in every hero's story. What I love is that instead of being surprised by yours, you'll expect them. Now, I know it may not be the most exciting part of the journey, but trust and believe it may be one of the most important. I believe that once we defeat our demons of doubt, fear, and personal insecurities, our individual monomyth's stage is set for the denouement. Well, what in the world is that? The final part of the narrative is when it is made clear that there will be a decisive victory and the victor will be you. Without the villain, the hero never reaches this point, but when they do nothing, it is the same. Preceding victory, all that's left is to bring back the knowledge, bestow the power, and grant passage to the hero following you.

You know that little boy we talked about earlier? Well, he has come quite a way from simply watching heroes on television. He's expanded his vision, found a sensei, traveled the world, changed his environment, beat the villain, and returned home. Today, his hero journey takes place in schools, at home, in churches, and through the keypads of computers and pads with ink pens. You see, not all heroes wear capes. They come in many sizes, colors, and forms. If you're reading this, I think you are one of them. So…are you ready, hero? If so, your journey awaits…

Points to Consider

1. How do you see the beginning of your hero journey? What do you think about your current environment, and what are your emotions about your current place in life because of it? Do you feel you have all the tools you need to begin now, or what do you feel is lacking?

2. Who do you go to for mentorship? Do you have great examples in your life to follow? If you do not have a mentor in your life at this moment, can you think of three people you could contact and ask to guide you? Could you imagine mentoring someone else at some point in your life?

3. What are some places that you have always dreamed of visiting? How possible do you think it is to get to this location? What are some closer places you feel you can visit within the next 6 months to a year? How do you think you will be different once you have visited this place?

4. How comfortable do you usually feel in new environments? Are you willing to change your living situation and the places

you are comfortable visiting to reach your goals? If you could move anywhere in the world tomorrow, where would that be?

5. Close your eyes and imagine how you would feel if you were in that special place right now. How would you stand, walk, talk, and operate? What would be different about you in that environment? Whatever your answers are to this section, try operating in that manner now from where you are.

6. What is the villain in your life? What is the one thing you feel is holding you back from where you need to be in life? How do you plan to face this obstacle one on one head up?

Reading Tips:

Often, people are advocating for increasing the amount of reading that we do, but not many are sharing suggestions on how to increase comprehension or retention of what you read to make it that much more of an enjoyable experience. Here I want to share a suggestion on HOW to read a book! You can use THIS book to practice, and then I want to challenge you to get three other books, try the method out, and see how you feel. Practice makes perfect.

When you first get your hands on a new book, I want you to go on a scouting mission. When you scout, you are just scoping out the landscape and seeing what's going on. You're not trying to read the book word for word at this stage. Let your eyes glance over the pages here and there. If there are pictures, slow down, bite, and give them the once over. Read the captions. Read over the table of contents. Read the about the author section. If it is a physical book, read the blurb on the inside jackets. Most times, they sum up the book to a large degree. Go through the book chapter for chapter and skim over the first and last paragraphs in the chapter. What is the point of this scout mission, you may ask? Time. You are seeing if THIS particular book is worth your time. Most of us have fast-paced lives, and only a small percentage of us take the time to sit down and read, to begin with. The last thing you want to do is take the time away from your PlayStation to read a book that sucks! These methods give you a great handle on what the book will be about, and this method also helps you to increase your reading speed if you decide to read the book because the subject matter won't be entirely new to you. You've seen this before. Take this reading tip and try it in your next book. Look for more tips like this in my future projects.

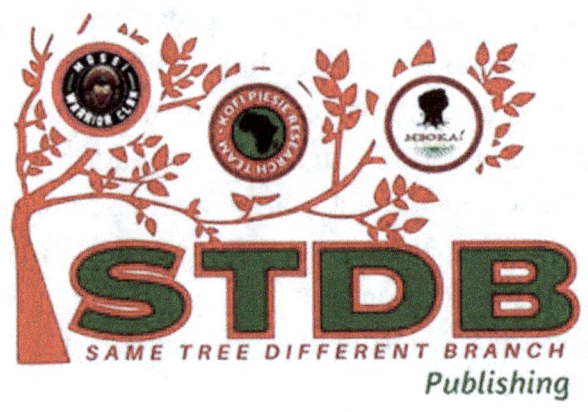

https://www.sametreedifferentbranchpublishing.com/

Office: 601-695-5797

Email: labarracenelson@yahoo.com

www.ingramcontent.com/pod-product-compliance
Lightning Source LLC
Chambersburg PA
CBHW052058230426
43662CB00036B/1370